The
WOMAN'S
BOOK *of*
GUARDIANS

The WOMAN'S BOOK *of* GUARDIANS

Divine Guides, Muses, Totems, *and* Protectors *for* Everyday Life

PEG STREEP

Inner Ocean Publishing
Maui, Hawai'i
San Francisco, California

Inner Ocean Publishing, Inc.
P.O. Box 1239
Makawao, Maui, HI 96768-1239
www.innerocean.com

Cover and book design by Suzanne Albertson

Publisher Cataloging-in-Publication Data
Streep, Peg.
The woman's book of guardians : divine guides, muses, totems,
and protectors for everyday life / by Peg Streep. — Maui Hawaii :
Inner Ocean, 2005.
p. ; cm.
Includes bibliographical references and index.
ISBN: 1-930722-43-5
1. Women and spiritualism. 2. Guides (Spiritualism)
3. Spiritual life. 4. Goddesses. 5. Spirituality. I. Title.
BF1275.W65 S77 2005
204/.4/082—dc22   0501

Printed on recycled paper

DISTRIBUTED BY PUBLISHERS GROUP WEST
For information on promotions, bulk purchases, premiums, or
educational use, please contact Special Markets: 866.731.2216
or sales@innerocean.com.

For Alexandra, my beloved daughter and
source of inspiration,
and for Craig, love of my life.

✌ CONTENTS ✌

Introduction   I

How to Use This Book   15

Part One ⌁ *Self*

Clarity • *Sarasvati*   37

Confidence • *The Lioness*   40

Courage • *Green Tara*   44

Creativity • *The Spider*   48

Discipline • *Athena*   53

Flexibility • *The Bird*   57

Generosity • *Lakshmi*   63

Groundedness • *Gaia*   66

Independence • *Epona*   69

Ingenuity • *Ariadne*   73

Intellect • *Themis*   77

Intention • *Isis*   80

Intuition • *Selene*   84

Joy • *The Three Graces*   87

Leadership • *Joan of Arc*   91

Productivity • *The Bee*   95

Self-Esteem • *The Amazon* 99
Spontaneity • *Artemis* 103
Transformation • *The Butterfly* 106

Part Two ᔆ *Relationship*

Choice • *Trivia* 113
Commitment • *Hestia* 117
Compassion • *Kuan Yin* 120
Divorce • *The Wolf* 124
Exploration • *The Dolphin* 128
Love • *Aphrodite* 131
Marriage • *Hera* 135
Motherhood • *The Virgin Mary* 139
Negotiation • *Ganesh* 143
Nurturance • *The Bear* 147
Partnership • *The Dyad* 151
Passion • *Pele* 155
Patience • *The Tortoise* 158
Reconciliation • *The Rainbow* 161
Sincerity • *Maat* 164
Support • *Penelope* 167

Contents

Part Three   *Body and Spirit*

Aging • *The Crane*		173
Energy • *The Tiger*		176
Fruitfulness • *Nut*		179
Future • *Jana*		182
Gratitude • *Flora*		186
Healing • *Hygeia*		190
Illumination • *Amaterasu Omikami*		193
Pleasure • *The Cat*		196
Renewal • *The Deer*		200
Simplicity • *Saint Thérèse of Lisieux*		205
Solace • *Demeter*		209
Spirituality • *Mary Magdalene*		213
Vision • *Fortuna*		218
Womanhood • *Changing Woman*		222
Acknowledgments		227
Bibliography		229
Index		235

✌ INTRODUCTION ∾

The room Diane has chosen for her office is tiny and holds only a few pieces of vintage furniture. In the seaside home she shares with her husband, this is her private space; painted in cream and white, it evokes a deliberate childlike simplicity. It is, as she puts it, a "place of innocence." A singer and writer, Diane is an inveterate collector of antiques, and her little room is filled with all manner of things to delight the eye and soul: small folk-art paintings, Victorian botanical drawings, her grandparents' wedding photo, a wood inlaid picture of a little girl carrying a doll that once hung in her mother's childhood bedroom. But the spiritual centerpiece is a nineteenth-century color lithograph of the goddess Lakshmi standing on a lotus, which Diane found in a New York City flea market. The lithograph was embellished by its previous owner with grain-painting on the frame and hand-painted lions on the matting. The print itself has been decorated with silks and flocked velvet, sequins and gold thread, beading and pearls on the goddess's sari and headdress.

Diane learned about Lakshmi from a close friend, and while the Hindu goddess of prosperity is often associated with wealth and material things, she feels Lakshmi represents "prosperity in the broadest sense." Diane looks upon Lakshmi's presence as an invitation to allow abundance into her life. On a jadeite plate, there is also a small statue of the Hindu god Ganesh—the remover of obstacles—as well as some coins, stones, and a postcard image of the Hindu goddess Sarasvati. Sarasvati is the goddess of wisdom as well as fertility and bountiful harvests; by extension, she too represents abundance. "If I can remove obstacles from my life," Diane comments, "and allow abundance into it, what more do I need?" In her purse, she carries a small image of Lakshmi to remind her to be open to possibilities when she is out in the world. There are other spiritual images in her home, including statues of the Buddha and Saint Cecelia, the patron saint of music and song. But the most significant guardian in Diane's life is the one she can neither see nor touch but whom she knows is there: the spirit of her mother who died when she was eight and who has always offered her protection.

In a New Jersey suburb, Luisa, a travel writer and mother of two, looks to Saint Thérèse of Lisieux for guidance. Her connection to the saint began during her first pregnancy when she was in danger of miscarrying and was confined to bed rest. Even though Luisa was a practicing Catholic, the saints had held little attraction until a close girlfriend introduced her to the story of Saint Thérèse, the "little flower." Saint Thérèse taught that spiritual devotion should be as simple, focused, and heartfelt as the earnest ardor young children bring to the things they love. This nineteenth-century saint died of tuberculosis at the age of twenty-four, after declaring, "My mission—to make God loved—will begin after my death. I will spend my heaven doing good on earth. I will let fall a shower of roses." In honor of the saint, Luisa's friend gave her a rosebush to plant for the baby who was about to be born. Luisa was understandably nervous about planting the gift—she knew that rosebushes can be finicky, and she worried about the negative symbolism if this one didn't thrive—but she decided to plant it anyway. The plant flourished, and her daughter was born healthy and full term. Luisa's connection to Saint Thérèse grew even stronger when, on the gray and chilly November day of her daughter's christening, a single rose bloomed in her otherwise moribund garden. Luisa understood this to be a sign and, following Saint Thérèse's example, tried to become more positive in outlook, less skeptical, and more, as she expressed it, "faithful." For over a decade, Luisa had incorporated meditation into her daily routine, and now,

Saint Thérèse's simple declaration of faith—to do the ordinary with extraordinary love—became her model. That inspiration has lasted more than a decade, and, according to Luisa, Saint Thérèse's guiding hand has often been visible in her life.

Claudia, an artist and retailer, has enjoyed a connection to Saint Thérèse for almost forty years, beginning at the age of seven when her mother gave her a picture of the saint. Claudia remembers that there was a statue of Saint Thérèse at her Catholic grade school, which she found beautiful; as Claudia got older, she was drawn to the tenets of the saint's "simple" faith, and she chose Therese as her confirmation name. Claudia wears tea-rose perfume in the saint's honor and has found that roses often figure in showing her which path to choose for the future. "It may be that I meet someone who is wearing a rose pin or perfume, or that I receive a greeting card which has roses on it," Claudia tells me. "Usually that means that there is an opportunity or possibility at hand. It may be connected to that person or it may mean that I need to take the initiative myself."

Debby, a fifty-four-year-old artist, recounts the journey that led her to discover the divine feminine, which she honors with both meditation and prayer before altars in her bedroom and kitchen. Debby was a stay-at-home mom in Little Rock, Arkansas, while her daughter and son, now in college, were growing up; she did volunteer work in the schools and the community. The journey that ultimately led her to the divine feminine began many years ago but took particular shape when she discovered the pantheon of Tibetan Buddhism seven years ago. Green Tara, who symbolizes compassion, became central to Debby's life, helping her with her fears and teaching her to have compassion for herself as she moved forward. In the Tibetan Buddhist tradition, Tara's name means "savior." Tara has twenty-one forms, each distinguished by a different color, iconography, and mission. The Green Tara is understood to be an emanation of the Buddha's compassion; confronted by the world's suffering, the Buddha worked long and hard to bring comfort to all. No sooner had he rested than he saw that the suffering continued, and a single tear dropped from his eye. Green Tara was born out of that tear. Debby recalls how saying Tara's mantra both comforted her and made her realize that she was on a healing path. Now, she says that mantra, among others, each morning, in front of lit candles on her altar. As she remarks, "The altars are around me to say, 'Remember who you are' and are a daily inspiration to remind me that I am held in her most precious arms."

My friend Nancy Blair, an artist and writer of numerous books on the ancient goddesses, counts Lilith, Inanna, and Kali as her most important guardians; she has reinterpreted them, peeling away the patriarchal overlay, to reveal how they embody the continuing cycles of nature. She recounts how, before she discovered the goddesses, she was lost and wandering: "I didn't see how I fit in the male world. I didn't have a female context or template; I had no guiding principles." Connecting to the goddesses was a wake-up call which permitted her to understand her own story, that of her mother, and those of other women in another context; it was, for her, a life-changing discovery in the truest sense.

The spiritual tradition I was raised in, Presbyterianism, included no saints or protectors, and I have found my own guardians through means both serendipitous and accidental. Not surprisingly, my guardians have been closely connected to the two important paths in my life, motherhood and writing. Although I had long collected images and portraits of women, my daughter's birth over seventeen years ago turned what had been an unconscious need for role models and guidance into a fully articulated one. As a woman who became a mother in her fourth decade of life, I looked for the threads that connected me to all the generations of women who had come before me, my spiritual foremothers, and discovered inspiration and wisdom in the stories of the ancient goddesses. That spiritual journey led to writing my first book, and, over time, one pathway led to another as I continued to research and explore sacred traditions. I began to see that these ancient stories—which I was once taught were no more than "myths" or "legends"—still held important and valuable lessons. Living in the modern, secular world, I marveled at how the sacred and the mundane were once closely connected in the West, and how, in the Eastern traditions, they still continue to be.

My interest in the goddesses led me to learn and then write about the Virgin Mary, who inherited many of the stories and symbols associated with the divine feminine. For over two thousand years, Mary has been the recipient of the prayers and hopes of the faithful, who sought in her a mother's love, compassion, protection, understanding, and solace. I worried that I could not do her justice, until one day—after writing a series of stories about Mary and her connection to flowers—my Victorian home filled up with ladybugs, the aphid-eating beetles that are named in her honor. Legend has it that in thirteenth-century

France, the harvest was threatened by swarms of aphids; the farmers prayed for the Virgin's intercession and woke the next morning to see their crops covered with the tiny, red, dotted beetles that devoured the pests, saving the harvest.

Try as we might to move them outdoors—my then seven-year-old daughter and I would ferry the ladybugs to the porch and yard on paper towels and cardboard, only to have them fly back in behind us—they nonetheless settled in for the end of the summer, the fall, and the winter. There were dozens and dozens of them—perhaps even hundreds and hundreds—in that big, rambling house. We saw them everywhere—on mantelpieces, windowsills, mirrors, near light fixtures—and they made all of us feel as though we were living in a peaceable kingdom. Even our bug-hunting cats left them alone. It was impossible to remain skeptical about the sign I'd been given, and no one in my family—not even my then husband, a man devoted to reason—doubted what had happened. The ladybugs took wing the following spring.

Now, in my apartment in New York City, images of various guardians watch over my daily life and inspire me to do the best I can with both the gifts I have been given and the obstacles life sometimes presents. A beautifully carved wood statue of the Buddha, a birthday gift from my child, sits on the window seat, emanating calm; he reminds me of the simple truths that belie the complexity of life, the quiet voice of wisdom that is louder than the din and bustle of the city streets below. A jade statue of Kuan Yin, goddess of compassion, stands next to the Buddha; I think she looks after me and helps me call upon my softer side after a hard day. In each room, there is an image of Ganesh, the remover of obstacles—and while my life is hardly obstacle free, he encourages me to believe that not one is insurmountable.

The large kitchen in my old home was the spiritual center of daily life—the house's soul—where I wrote my books and made phone calls, where my daughter did her homework and ate snacks after school with her friends, where I prepared our meals and we ate. In that house, the windowsills above my stove held statuary, animal totems, and plants—an altar to the daily routines of nurturance performed by women the world over. My New York kitchen is tiny and windowless, no more than a closet; it is a space pared down to the essentials needed to cook and clean up. But, even in this space, with the guardians' help, I can remember that the preparation of food is filled with sacral intent and that "feeding" my daughter—literally and spiritually—with the gifts of the earth defines motherhood. Images of mothers—Demeter, the Greek earth goddess of the grain; two of the Virgin Mary; and a reproduction of the Goddess of Laussel, the moon's horn in her hand—surround me. A tiny mounted Ganesh has an offering bowl filled with rice.

The way of the guardians is an ancient, well-trodden path. Guardian spirits, supernatural entities closely connected to human destiny, appear in different forms in all cultures and spiritual traditions the world over. Their ubiquity speaks both to a primal, essential human need to feel protected and guided and to the fragility and precariousness of the human condition. If nothing else, guardians underscore the yearning to feel that we do not travel alone as we undertake the journey of life. On another level, guardian traditions reflect the difficulty of establishing an individual identity that is both consciously chosen and righteous in intent. Guardian spirits—whether they are called *genii*, *lares*, angels, goddesses, gods, spirit guides, or saints—are sources of inspiration and self-realization, as well as help and protection. This common thread links traditions that are otherwise meaningfully different, yielding a tapestry that reveals much about our shared humanity and spiritual concerns.

As early as the Paleolithic Era and probably before, human beings sought to invoke, summon, thank, and, sometimes, appease the spirits that were thought to govern the physical world. While the precise meaning of the symbols and animals painted onto the walls of Paleolithic caves may elude us, the paintings as well as the female statues now known as "goddesses" clearly attest to a belief in a numinous reality capable of affecting and changing the reality of this world. Later, more complex systems of belief—which, in time, became the basis of mythology and folklore—make it clear that no detail of human life was too small or insignificant not to have a presiding guardian to whom acts of propitiation were due.

In most cultures, fierce, other-worldly guardians stood watch over all things valuable and mysterious. While the dragon Ladon who never slept as protected the golden apples of immortality, dragons breathing fire kept the gold of the Nibelungs safe. For the Egyptians, the realm of the dead—the place to which no human could bear testimony—was presided over by the dreaded Ammut. A creature with a crocodile's head, lion's forelimbs, and hippopotamus's trunk and legs, she not only guarded the netherworld but also meted out justice; those whose hearts were weighed down by guilt were consumed by her and deprived of the afterlife. Cerberus—the snarling, three-headed dog of Hades for the Greeks—became even more gruesome in Roman times, when pictured with fifty heads, a dragon's tail, and serpents along his back. In the Nordic realm, the fierce wolves of Odin were the netherworld's guardians.

The world over, far gentler but sometimes demanding guardians protected the loci of everyday life: the entrance to the home; the fork in the road; the peaks of the mountains; the waters of streams, rivers, and seas; the skies and the earth. They presided over the metaphorical and literal junctures of the human life cycle—birth, the passage from childhood to adulthood, marriage, sickness and health, and, finally, death—and could provide protection and guidance. Everything that provided sustenance and nurturance to humanity had a guardian spirit, a god or goddess, responsible for it—the fire in the hearth, the animal hunted and slaughtered, the goat or calf herded, the seed planted and harvested, the rains and floods that watered the crops, the tree felled—who was to be thanked and honored.

In most cultures, an individual's destiny could not be fully achieved without the help of a guardian spirit; in fact, a life lived without dignity and honor was often ascribed to the influence of a malevolent spirit. The Romans believed that all things animate and inanimate—including humans, animals, places—were possessed of indwelling spirits *(numen)*; these spiritual presences were part of daily life and were honored by offerings. For example, the *Lares Familiares* took care of the house and household, while the *Penates* guarded the larder; the hearth was sacred to Vesta, and the doors and entrances to Janus. Each individual life was directed by a guiding spirit—a *genius* for men, a *juno* for women—which exercised important influence on both character and destiny. The *genius* or *juno* was honored on the individual's birthday. Cities, colonies, provinces, armies, and even localities had *genii*—as did the professions.

In most of the Native American cultures, the gifts of the guardian weren't bestowed at birth but were discovered and earned at puberty. Young men participated in rituals or vision quests to acquire a guardian spirit, as would young women isolated during their first menses.

Even though the monotheistic vision of Judeo-Christianity banished the gods, goddesses, and spirits who had once tended to every aspect of life, the need for guardian protection expressed itself in other ways. The Old Testament and Judaism preserved the tradition of the guardian angel, while cultural practices such as naming preserved the idea of the spirit guardian; Jewish children are often named after an admired deceased family member in hopes that the child will emulate his or her virtues and follow his or her example. In Christianity, the saints and martyrs of the early Church became the guardians and intercessors to the living, as did the angels and the Virgin Mary.

The guardians in this book are a bouquet gathered from the gardens of many traditions and, admittedly, reflect my own preferences and tastes. There are many more guardians who could have been included in these pages, and if you would like to research some of these, please go to the bibliography.

Finally, the guardians are offered to help you through hard times and challenges, and to keep you strong and of good cheer through every day. Learning about and understanding these ancient models can sometimes help you open doors that might otherwise stay shut.

∼ HOW TO USE THIS BOOK ∼

The guardians in this book are offered as a way of helping you get around the surmountable obstacles that sometimes block you from doing what you want and need. No matter what you call these obstacles—ambivalence or indecision; lack of focus, vision, or commitment; timidity, fear, or insecurity; or inertia—they can all have the same effect. Each can stop you in your tracks.

The guardians can help, but there is one condition. The key to the process is your self-awareness and your willingness to work so that your guardians can guide you.

What do I mean by "work"? Let me give you an example. Over the years, I've noticed a pattern when I'm asked what I do for a living. Usually, when I explain that I'm a writer, the person responds, "Oh, I've had an idea for a book forever but I've never gotten around to it," or, "I would write if I only had the time." I've come to understand that what prompts this response is that everyone knows how to write. While I'd like to think that what distinguishes me from those who only think about writing is my brilliance and scintillating wit, I fear it's much simpler than all that. It's really about work.

What really differentiates me from the person with the idea she never got on the page is that I actually sit down at my computer every day and write. Sometimes what I turn out is good and publishable, and the work is actually pleasurable—and sometimes it's not. How I feel on any given day and where the writing ends up are beside the point, because I have decided that I want to be a writer and to make my living doing it. I can't be a writer without sitting down at the computer every day and writing. *That's* the work.

On the flip side, there are many other areas in my life I've wanted to enrich and change, but, somehow, the work never gets started or, if it does, grinds to a halt. For years, when I lived in the suburbs, I would start the work of gardening with a flurry of planning and activity. I'd begin by piling the kitchen high with garden catalogues; then I'd fill the windowsills and tabletops with little seedlings planted in peat pots. Late spring would find me digging the dirt, turning over the soil. I would weed and nurture the perennials and plant countless annuals. But, inevitably, by the midsummer months, I'd be in the middle of a book—once it was actually a book about gardening—and my little paradise would be largely forgotten. There were always different reasons but the result was always the same.

I'd spend the rest of the summer jealously eyeing the gardens of friends and strangers who hadn't stopped their work and whose gardens were in glorious and full flower.

Mind you, there's nothing wrong with not doing the work—*as long as you don't care about the outcome.* Over time, I learned that I cared about my garden—but not as much as I cared about other things in my life. And those other things are the ones I continue to work on.

Doing the work—that's where the guardians can help. The guardians aren't meant to be reserved only for truly *big* life changes and decisions—such as changing careers, beginning a new relationship, moving cross-country, having a baby, or ending a marriage. Unless your life is very different from mine or those of the people I know, small things—those "the guppies are eating me alive" things— can get in your way and stop you in your tracks just as often as the big ones can. Sometimes, the little things—like getting up the energy to organize my work space, return a phone call I've been dreading, or finish something I started weeks or even months ago—seem to swamp every inner resource I have, and I end up not doing what I need to. Sometimes, just a small amount of negativity or hesitation has prevented me from following up on an opportunity or idea that could actually have changed a part of my life for the better. Luckily, the guardians are always more than happy to help.

The "work" of changing yourself and your life can take many forms, and in the pages that follow, I've offered suggestions for how you can work with your guardians to use them to their full advantage. You should choose the path that makes you most comfortable and that yields the most benefits for you, or a combination of several.

The Basics

Begin by choosing a place for the work you are going to do with your guardians. If possible, it should be a neutral place in your home, unassociated with career or unfinished chores or the more demanding or difficult aspects of your life. Most importantly, it needs to be yours—one small piece of your living space that is yours alone, where neither you nor the guardians you use to do your work will be disturbed. Choose your space with your own comfort in mind; make room for a chair or a pillow for meditation. Clean and straighten it before you begin. If you plan on using representations of your guardians—statues or pictures—you may want to choose a space near a windowsill, shelf, or tabletop. You can work outside if the climate permits and if there is enough peace and quiet.

Make time for the work you intend to do, and honor your intention by giving—your wholehearted attention. Turn on your answering machine, and turn off your cell phone. If you know that you'll be interrupted, find another time.

Representations of your guardians can take any form. You can draw a picture or even create a sculpture from the fast-drying clays available at craft stores. You can also photocopy an image from a library book or you can acquire a representation from the many vendors who sell statuary on the Internet. In some of the guardian entries that follow, I suggest using symbolic representations—a piece of string, for example, as the emblem of Ariadne's ingenuity or a feather for the lessons Maat teaches—but you can also work without representations, relying on your imagination to provide the imagery. Personally, I have found that having a concrete object at hand—a picture of a goddess, a statue, an animal fetish, or an amulet or stone as a stand-in—helps me focus more clearly. I also use portable imagery—often in the form of a pendant on a necklace or a small, pocket-sized piece—because it helps me realize the guardian's presence no matter what I am doing. The choice is yours.

Keep the space free and clear of distractions. If it is a windowsill or shelf, remove anything extraneous to the work you are planning to do. If you have decided to work without representations, make sure that the objects on which your eyes will rest are either neutral or provide a focal point.

Spend a bit of time in the area you have chosen to assess its energy *and*, most importantly, its effect on you. Is it light and airy enough? Does this area of your home lift your spirits or does it make you feel dull and tired? Do you feel focused or distracted? I find that the greenery of plants—the presence of the life force—automatically raises the energy level in a room, particularly during the winter months on the East Coast where I live. Remember that you don't need an exotic or flowering plant to raise the energy level; a low-light plant such as a pothos or an ivy will serve the purpose just as well.

Following are some of the approaches you may want to incorporate while you work with your guardians. You can use these in sequence if you like—moving from meditation to visualization to prayer to affirmation, for example—or you can simply focus on one. Above all, *remember to take your time*. Don't expect a single session with the guardians to work a miracle; they can only help you work toward one.

Meditation: Remember that a meditation is deep, sustained thought, free of other distractions. Meditation is not necessarily goal oriented and shouldn't be confused with problem solving or thinking something "through." If anything, meditation is nonlinear thought; it is reflective, closed, and continuous. The meditative process is internal; if you wish to visualize it, think of the motion of the ripples caused by a stone thrown into a pond. They move out in circles, quietly, slowly. Picture your thoughts flowing in the same pattern.

Try to prepare yourself by ridding yourself of other concerns. Make time for your meditation; it does not have to be long, but it does need to be *quiet*. Get your other concerns, chores, and phone calls out of the way first; it's impossible to let yourself meditate if a part of you is listening for the phone. Wear comfortable clothes that let you breathe and move without binding; I've yet to meet a woman who can meditate in tight jeans. Relax your body and take some deep breaths; shake the tension out of your hands and legs. Light a candle, both for the scent and for the symbolism of illumination.

Let your mind do the work. Begin by concentrating on one aspect of the guardian, and then let your mind make the next connection for you. You will learn from the associations you make when you are quiet and focused.

Once you are comfortable with the process, you may find it useful to take small breaks to meditate during the working day—even for just a few minutes. Bringing the guardians into your thoughts has a way of energizing and invigorating the spirit.

Visualization: This approach is extremely useful if you have difficulty acting on your impulses or if you tend to second-guess yourself. Focus on the guardian and bring your mind to bear on the strengths she embodies and symbolizes. Visualization is much more linear and ana-lytical than meditation, but like meditation, it is less about *outward* communication than it is about honing your own inner senses.

The process of visualization is a bit like watching water run off into soil. As the water flows, it begins to shape the soil—first creating grooves and then other, smaller tributaries. As the water moves more soil, its flow speeds up, and the patterns it creates in the soil become more complex. Its ability to transform the soil actually increases. Visualization works the same way.

Begin by visualizing one of the guardians; open up your mind and actually see her. Take your time. Try to make your mental image of the guardian as complete as possible. If you are working with a female guardian, give her a face, a voice, clothes, a stride. If you are working with an animal spirit, give the spirit as much physical presence as you possibly can. If the spirit is a bird, for example, focus on her wings, her feathers, her shape in the air, her colors. Imagine her taking flight against the sky or sitting among the branches of the trees. If you are musically inclined, allow yourself to "hear" her song.

Now picture the guardian in the situation you are faced with. Work on truly understanding the characteristics the guardian embodies. Try to understand these qualities in depth by asking yourself questions: How does compassion manifest itself? What do you mean by strength?

The next step involves visualizing yourself as embodying the characteristics of the guardian and, if you are concerned with a specific problem, visualizing the situation itself. First, try to imagine the situation as fully and completely as you can. If what you need to accomplish requires you to confront or question some- one else, call up your body language and voice. Will you move with confidence or hesitance? Bring to mind the words you might use. Imagine yourself listening to those words, and decide if they will bring about what you wish to happen.

If, on the other hand, your goal is to strengthen a character trait—to become more courageous or com- passionate, more open or cooperative, for example— visualize your guardian exhibiting that trait. Then, think about how possessing that trait in fullness would change your life. Once again, envision yourself in as detailed a way as possible.

Writing can help make visualization even more concrete.

Writing and Journaling: Writing can be used as a spiri- tual tool when working with your guardians, either as an aid to meditation and visualization or on its own. If you've been keeping a journal, this approach might be the easiest, but if writing hasn't been part of your life, take a deep breath and relax before you put pen to paper. First and foremost, remember that *no one is grad-*

ing you when you write! Many people who are unaccustomed to writing more than a business letter or a short thank-you note tend to freeze up when they start. Don't worry about your style—or how good the words "look" on the page. This writing is for you—and you alone. Writing down what appear to be "random" thoughts can reveal a pattern otherwise hidden from view, words on the page can help clarify and articulate both our thoughts and feelings.

You can use a special notebook when you're working with your guardians (particularly if you are writing down personal thoughts that you want to keep private), or you can use small slips of paper. These slips of paper can also be used in other kinds of guardian work; see the entry on "Compassion" for an example.

There is no "right" way of using writing as a spiritual tool to connect with your guardians. Experiment with putting pen to paper, and see how expressing your thoughts makes you feel. If writing full sentences throws you off track, start by writing phrases or even single words. Don't be judgmental about what you have written. Once again, give the process time—there's no benefit to working quickly.

If you need the guardians to resolve a long-term

problem or issue in your life, try writing in the form of a journal, and date all of your entries. Over time, your journal entries will reveal the evolution of your thoughts and will help you understand the underlying issues you need to confront. Each time you go back to your journal, reread what you've written in the previous entry and take a deep breath. Think about where you were and what you wrote before for at least five minutes before you begin a new entry.

Storytelling: Once-sacred stories told by successive generations are the source for what we know about the guardians contained in this book. The guardians remind us that human beings are born into a world of story and always have been—even before the invention of writing. Now, as then, stories help shape our identities as members of societies and families, as well as individuals. In addition to sacred stories drawn from the Bible and other spiritual works, the stories that shape and influence us include those told by our parents and other relatives about our origins and childhood histories, those we tell our friends and loved ones about ourselves when we set out into the world on our own, and those we tell our children in turn. Both the stories we tell and those we choose not to tell are filled with meaning.

Our contemporary society is so supersaturated with meaningless stories, the din of narratives pertaining to celebrities and the would-be famous—in newspapers, magazines, books, and movies; on television and the Internet—that it's easy to forget the power of story. But the true power of stories to inspire and guide us remains constant. Think of each of the guardian stories in this volume as merely a beginning, and allow yourself to extrapolate from them. You can add details or even rewrite them in your own words. You can weave your own and your guardian's stories together, embellishing each as you see fit. Use your storytelling gifts to connect with the guardians in poetry, prose, phrases, or drawings. This doesn't have to be a private activity—the tradition includes an audience, after all—and you can bring yourself closer to your guardian by telling her story to someone else.

Prayer: Unlike meditation, the flow of prayer is outward; if meditation moves in the circular motion of a stone thrown into a pond, then prayer flows like a stream, from a point within to a point outside the self. A prayer is an entreaty or an earnest request or a petition. Understanding what we are asking of our guardians—moving through and then completing the meditative or contemplative process—leads naturally to the prayer itself.

You can make up your own prayers or use the recommended anthologies in the bibliography as resource. Some of the guardian entries include specific prayers as well.

Affirmation: Ancient rituals pertaining to guardians usually included incantations as well as words of praise, and many people find that addressing the guardian directly during the course of their work connects them to the guardian's spirit even more closely. I have given examples of affirmations in some of the guardian entries, but you should feel free to use your own words. Affirmations bolster self-confidence and feelings of security; like prayers, they flow outward but also connect the spirit within to the world of action.

Creating Sacred Space: Building an altar is, for many women, both a way of honoring the intention to change and a way of acknowledging the presence of the guardian in their lives. While certain traditions, such as Tibetan Buddhism, prescribe the objects to be placed on the altar, I regard altar building as a creative activity in which the individual chooses how to manifest spirit in a physical form. For examples of ways to create sacred space, please see the "Tiger" entry.

Working with the Guardians

Life is a process, and the woman living it is always changing and growing. Your short-term focus shifts from day to day, week to week, month to month, as you face different goals and challenges. For your guardian work on what prove to be essentially temporary situations—preparing for a big business meeting, getting the house in order for a family visit, supporting a friend in a crisis, for example—you may wish to work with the guardians as simply as possible.

Should you decide to work with representational objects, you should put your guardian material away in a safe place after you've accomplished your goal. Remember that sometimes the pattern of short-term challenges tends to reveal itself as consistent, and there may well come a time when these "short-term" issues reveal themselves to be "long-term" ones in disguise.

Long-term work is another matter entirely; the easiest path is the well-worn one. Keep the guardians and your work space intact until you feel the work has actually been accomplished. I surround myself with my most important guardians for ongoing inspiration, but you may want to put yours away in a special place (a designated drawer or box) until you feel the need to call upon them again.

Learning from the Guardians

Perhaps the best way of describing how to learn from the guardians is to give an example of how they don't work.

Every summer there's always at least one commercial on television that shows a dreary, sad-looking, flowerless garden—full of weeds, drooping bushes, and lifeless, burned-out grass. As it happens, this is a commercial for plant food promising, of course, that help is on the way. No sooner has the spokesman wielding plant food fed this sorry lawn than the color on the screen changes from dull and lifeless to bursting with vigor! Magically, the grass turns verdant, the roses bloom, and the flower beds fill with beauty.

Anyone who buys plant food hoping for that kind of

transformation is clearly either hopelessly gullible or, to put it more kindly, out of touch with how nature works. But people buy self-help books all the time, expecting to effect changes in themselves that will be just as instantaneous—seeking a Viagra for the soul.

The guardians can't change your personality or character overnight. They also can't guide you without your help and energy. Change takes thought, effort, and commitment on your part; on their part, the guardians will provide an example, support, and inspiration.

What the guardians do best is help you understand yourself and your potential in new and valuable ways. They can help you tap into aspects of yourself that you haven't fully explored.

Human beings operate on both a literal and symbolic level; we are affected by symbolic messages all the time, whether we are conscious of their effect or not. These messages—both positive and negative—are communicated by the larger society we live in; by the books, magazines, and newspapers we read; by the images in the movies and television we watch; and by the words and gestures of our friends and enemies, coworkers and strangers, children and spouses. Negative imagery affects us by lowering our self-esteem, making us anxious about our abilities, and depressing us in every sense of the word. Positive imagery, on the other hand, lifts us up.

Working with the guardians—choosing our own symbols—permits us to use our innate abilities to their fullest advantage by surrounding ourselves with positive, empowering, and energizing imagery. The guardians permit us to see ourselves more clearly when we've been blocked by the ways—some of them stereotypes that we inherited from our culture, others learned during our upbringings— in which we think about ourselves, our actions, and our goals.

During the almost twenty years I have been writing about, researching, and working with ancient imagery and the mythology of the feminine, the guardians have emerged as a positive way of looking at myself and my own life. The complexity of the guardians has reminded me not to be simplistic about either my shortcomings or my talents. Hestia, the goddess of the hearth, has taught me much about the importance of "home" and why housework— an activity I always face with a heavy heart—is symbolic of commitment and central to spiritual health. In a different way, Artemis has helped me realize that not everything in my heart need be rational or tame; there is room for wilderness in all of us. The guardians have energized me when I feel low and connected me to my feminine history when I feel up. Most importantly, I have, over time, learned from their examples.

The guardians give us another context in which to tell our own stories and, by understanding them in different ways, to shape them anew. That is a subtle but meaningful gift.

Choosing Your Own Guardians

The guardians presented in this book can be used in different combinations and for other purposes than those I describe, and you should feel free to choose different guardians from different sections for your own work. If the associations you bring to a specific guardian are different from those I have offered on these pages, work with your own; after all, the guardian is *yours*.

Self

Clarity
Sarasvati

In Hinduism, Sarasvati was once a river goddess whose cool waters brought life to the land, and thus she has ancient connections to fertility and abundance; although her eponymous river has long since disappeared, her name "The One That Flows" preserves her origins. It seems likely that long ago her sacred waters purified and cleansed the bodies and souls of ritual bathers, as other rivers in India do today. Consort of the creator Brahma, she was later identified with the goddess of speech, Vac, or "sound," as well as with music; she is often shown playing a lute or a stringed instrument. But Sarasvati—pictured as a beautiful woman with two or more arms, seated upon a swan, peacock, or lotus—is now primarily understood as the embodiment of speech, intellect, and thought. White— the emblem of purity and clarity—is her color. In the Rig-Veda, she is described as "Sarasvati, the mighty flood/ illuminates with light/ She brightens every thought."

We appeal to Sarasvati when memory no longer serves us, when we can't think straight, when we're running in circles or we've actually lost the forest for the trees. These phrases have become clichés because there is truth in them.

The "word" is sacred to Sarasvati. Through her we can begin to grasp that clarity and articulation go hand in hand and that we must give voice to our true selves. To call on Sarasvati, clear your mind of the extraneous by meditating or by listening to music that calms and centers you. Visualize yourself walking through a shallow stream; imagine the cool waters rising and splashing against your legs as your feet sink into the soft silt and mud. If you were to look down at that very moment, you'd see that the water has become cloudy. Then again, if you stood perfectly still, the water would return to crystalline clarity. Metaphorically, that is the mental and emotional still point you need to reach.

Make time to read a book on a subject that promises to stimulate or interest you; it can be poetry, fiction, or nonfiction. Keep a written record of your thoughts and responses to what you've read. Nurture your intellect and let the "word" come forth.

Your journal will help you bring the clarity Sarasvati represents into your life. Begin a rhythm of writing every day; free-associate so that you can begin to tease out the connections that are temporarily hidden. Work at finding the right word or words to describe your feelings and thoughts. Before you go to bed, ask yourself a single question that fits your situation—"Why does this worry me?" or "Is this what I want?"—and answer it in your journal when you wake up. The bright light of early morning is the best time to welcome Sarasvati's wisdom.

Confidence
The Lioness

The human connection to the lion and lioness is ancient; almost twenty thousand years ago, in the sacred cave of Trois Frères in France, a portrait of a lioness was etched onto the walls—majestic and powerful. Twelve thousand years later, from Çatal Hüyük, a statue depicts a goddess giving birth on a throne of lionesses—an association that would continue for millennia. Female divinities were pictured riding or seated on lions, as emblems of physical and spiritual power closely connected to the sun and solar energy. A fourth-century BCE Greek statue of the goddess Cybele, the great mother of the gods, shows her cradling a lion in her lap as if it were a domestic cat. Lions drew Cybele's chariot through the streets of Rome in a holy procession. Lions were pictured as the companions of Ishtar, Isis, and Artemis; in fact, the holy procession dedicated to Artemis was led by a lioness. The connection between the divine feminine and the lioness remained vibrant since, a thousand years later, the Virgin Mary was pictured as sitting on a lion-headed throne or with tamed lions at her feet.

While the lioness embodies strength and confidence, she also reflects the destructive potential inherent in both qualities. The Egyptian goddess Sekmet had the head of a lioness; while she was invoked as a healer and a guardian of the underworld, she was also the goddess of war and destruction, closely associated with the burning heat of the sun. Sekmet reminds us that untrammeled confidence can become a destructive force when it crosses the line and becomes egotism or self-justification.

In nature, the lioness is a skilled hunter but rarely hunts alone; she works with the other females in the pride, most of which are her blood relatives, to increase her chances of success. She teaches that confidence in our abilities isn't based in a vacuum and that it is rarely achieved without a support system of some kind. Even though the males in the pride do not actively hunt—that is the females' job— the lioness cedes her kill first to the male, who not only takes what we call "the lion's share" but also makes sure the cubs get to eat. Only then does the lioness eat—a parable, perhaps, of how confidence can't depend on either a sense of entitlement or the need to be "first."

The lioness embodies healthy confidence, which is not born out of bravado or empty gestures, but is based in a real, life-tested sense of self that includes knowledge of both our strengths and limitations. There's a wonderful fable attributed to Aesop, often told to small children, but which contains a valuable lesson for adults as well. One day, a small mouse looking for food skittered across the paw of a sleeping lion and woke him. Annoyed, the lion picked up the mouse and opened his mouth wide, intending to eat him. The mouse begged for mercy, apologizing for his accidental affront, and finally, in desperation, promised, "If you spare me, I'll be eternally grateful and will, one day, return the favor in kind." The lion roared with laughter—what help could a mouse offer a lion, after all?—but decided to let him go nonetheless. Sometime later, the lion fell into a snare set by hunters; entangled in ropes, he roared with anger and frustration. The mouse heard him and recognized the roaring of "his" lion—and, as he had promised, came running. He gnawed through the ropes and set the lion free.

Invite Lioness into your life by turning off that internal critic—the one who only sees what you can't do—and by focusing on the areas in which you are strong but could be stronger still. Use your journal to explore what makes you feel unsure about yourself, looking at both the past and the present. Studies have shown that women and men have different levels of self-confidence *and* different ways of dealing with issues of confidence. Women ruminate more about what they aren't good at and tend to worry over a failure or setback; in addition, perhaps because of the way they are brought up, they also tend to underestimate their own abilities and accomplishments and to underplay them in front of peers. Becoming proactive about a single aspect of your life— committing yourself to getting into better physical shape, taking a specialized course to broaden an area of expertise, or learning something totally new—can charge up your self-confidence.

Do use the power of affirmation every day and become your own inner cheerleader. Saying the words out loud— "I *can* do this" or "I *will* be able to accomplish my goal"— can make all the difference. Concentrate on seeing your successes and failures in a meaningful context, remembering that neither success nor failure is ever total. In every success, there is always room for growth and improvement; in every failure, there are always areas of success. Look at not only the accomplishments you've achieved on your own but also the successes of others to which you have contributed.

For another point of view, see the "Self-Esteem" entry.

Courage
Green Tara

A powerful, dynamic, and multifaceted goddess, Green Tara is the guardian and intercessor who can free us from fears and anxieties so that a stronger, more courageous self can emerge into the world. For women whose courage may be circumscribed by their sense of what constitutes "womanly" or "female" behavior—a result of upbringing or cultural pressure—Green Tara can be especially helpful.

Her name in Sanskrit means "star," and she represents the fixed stars by which sailors navigated; she is a guardian of the literal and metaphorical journey between two points, keeping the traveler safe and on the right path. Her name is also linked to the Sanskrit root *tri*, meaning "to carry across" or "to save"; in Tibet she is known as "She Who Saves." This pure and sublime goddess is usually pictured with her left leg folded beneath her in the contemplative position; her right leg, though, is extended so that she can spring into action quickly and decisively. She is associated with quick thinking and spontaneity, and her green skin color signifies growth, vigor, energy, and activity. She is usually dressed in silk finery and much jewelry, indicating that she is of this world.

Two different stories of Tara's origins illuminate her essential nature. The first is that she was born out of the tear shed by the Buddha of Compassion, Avalokiteshvara, when he became aware that, despite all of his interventions, the world was still full of suffering. Tara was instantly manifested on a blue lotus floating on the tear. The second story paints a picture of Tara as strong, self-possessed, and feisty. In a previous incarnation, Tara was the daughter of a king. She made offerings and prayed for thousands and thousands and thousands of years—no one knows precisely how long—until she became fully enlightened. Because her offerings and prayers had been matchless, the monks, wishing to acknowledge her awakening, told her that they would pray for her to be changed into a man so that she could spread the teachings of Buddha. But Tara disagreed, answering that life held no distinction between "male" and "female" and that clinging to this distinction was both worthless and a delusion. Instead, she acknowledged that there were many who sought to spread enlightenment in the body of a man but few who wished to follow the path in the female form. She vowed to bring the teachings to all as a female until the end of time. Above all, Green Tara affirms us in our feminine nature.

This goddess's power was understood to be so strong and immediate that simply invoking her name was thought to conquer each of the following eight fearsome realities and their symbolic equivalents: lions (pride), wild elephants (delusions), forest fires (hatred), snakes (envy), brigands (fanatical views), prisons (avarice), floods (lust), and demons (doubts).

Let Green Tara help you confront your fears and anxieties by bringing them to the light of day. Remind yourself of how the goddess stood up to the monks and recognize that what sometimes passes for "common wisdom" about behaviors or attitudes or even women's roles may not be "wisdom" at all. Green Tara symbolizes action and energy; try not to overanalyze what's holding you back from confronting the person or situation you need to deal with. Keep in mind that just a little belief— such as repeating again and again "I *can* do this"—often goes a very long way. Energize yourself with activity; exercise on a regular basis to feel physically empowered. Take a brisk walk in the morning, join a gym, or take a dance class. Pay attention to what and how much you are eating; use food as fuel. Make sure that your surroundings make you feel spirited, not listless or lethargic.

Do what you can to make your home brighter and lighter; remove curtains that block the sun and get rid of clutter. A fresh coat of paint will do wonders to revitalize a room, as will adding plants, a fountain, or some bright-colored accents such as pillows. Throw out old newspapers and magazines to ensure that you are surrounded by Green Tara's energy. Remember that you are following the path of a deity ready to spring into action.

Creativity
The Spider

Glistening by the light of the moon and the sun, her gossamer web of perfectly realized circles and spirals, lines and squares epitomized divine pattern. She wove something of nothing, and in the eyes of the ancients, the spider's art was nothing less than the story of all creation, albeit on a smaller scale. She was perceived as uniquely feminine because, like the female of every species, she could bring forth substance, life, and relationship out of her body, where there had been nothing before. This powerful metaphor for the creative force gave humanity the symbolic vocabulary for many of life's processes. The spun thread was emblematic of the life span—created, measured, and cut by a divine spinner who was sometimes the weaver herself. That which is woven, these sacred stories tell us, can also be ripped out.

Weaving is an emblem of cohesion and relationship between formerly separate individuals or entities, as well as life itself. Because weaving requires forethought—the ability to visualize the object to be created from the very start—many of the goddesses connected to weaving are associated with words, thoughts, dreams, and songs. In almost every culture, the spider's art becomes the province of a goddess or deity who embodies the female creative principle.

Spider encourages us to see our creativity not as an isolated talent, something separate from the everyday activities of life, but as part and parcel of it. We tend to see "art" and "artistry" as elevated above mundane activities, but Spider tells us otherwise. Evidence of the artist within each and every one of us can be seen in all that we do, glinting threads in the tapestry of life. Spider also encourages us to see our femaleness as a potent wellspring for the creative force. Elizabeth Wayland Barber, a scholar of textiles and weaving, asked why spinning, sewing, and weaving had been the provenance of women for millennia. Her answer was both simple and profound: these arts fit easily into a life based on multiple tasks, including the need to watch over and care for children.

The spider and her art have had many incarnations the world over. The ancient Egyptians imagined that the goddess Neith, a weaver's shuttle on her head, created the world through realization and naming. Her voice wove the web of creation. Similarly, the Native American Keres

Spider Woman—whose name, according to scholar Paula Gunn Allen, means "Creating-Through-Thinking-Woman"—brought forth creation by thinking, dreaming, singing, and naming. For the Greeks, the woven fabric was Athena's gift, while the Moirai, or Fates, spun, measured, and cut the thread of life. The Romans called the Fates either *Fata,* from the Latin for "that which is spoken," or the Parcae, from the Latin for "giving birth." In Scandinavia, they were the Norns. In Japan, the goddess of the sun, Amaterasu Omikami, had a loom that wove the events of the cosmos.

Allow yourself to see your creativity in new terms. Remember that "weaving" can be both literal and metaphorical and that building and maintaining relationships are important aspects of creativity.

Try to acknowledge that ordinary tasks can be infused with creativity. Take care setting the table for a meal, adding small touches such as candles or a vase filled with flowers. Learn a new recipe, keeping in mind that preparing food is a creative act. Serving food also builds the web of connection.

Encourage your creative self by writing in your journal every day and experimenting a bit. Don't self-criticize; let your inner artist emerge by writing about anything you wish. Try your hand at describing someone or something of beauty or meaning, and let that, in turn, lead you to begin another imaginative thread.

Build an altar to acknowledge your own inner artist. Use images of connection and relationship—photographs, gifts you've been given, mementos—to honor that aspect of Spider in your life. Use woven or braided objects to symbolize the fabric of creation. If you already know a handicraft such as knitting or crocheting, make something for your altar. This might also be the perfect time to learn a craft; try Deborah Bergman's book, *The Knitting Goddess*, for example. Braiding—using threads, ribbons, yarn, leather strings, or even scarves—is an easy way to express your creativity. Make cards with inspirational words and quotations to put on your altar; you can use your own words or those of others. One of my favorite quotations is from Georgia O'Keeffe, the American painter, whose words tell us much about what an artist does:

> Nobody sees a flower—really—it is so small—we haven't time—and to see it takes time like a friend takes time. If I could paint a flower exactly as I see it no one would see what I see because I would

paint it small like the flower is small. So I said to myself—I'll paint what I see—what the flower is to me but I'll paint it big . . .

Art lets us see connections—the hidden web beneath—that we otherwise might not see. Put a flower on your altar and take time to see it—just as you would take time to "see" the essence of a friend—and let your inner weaver come forth.

Discipline
Athena

Of all the Greek goddesses, the helmeted Athena seems, at first, the most detached from the sacred feminine since her mother, Metis, a goddess of wisdom, never bore her. Not only did Athena emerge full-blown from her father Zeus's head, but she remained a virgin (*parthenos*), unconnected to either fertility or the earth. But the gray-eyed Athena, counselor to the hero and goddess of the battle won through strategy, was her mother's daughter, after all; she embodied *metis*, the wisdom that is firmly rooted in the real world and yields practical results.

Different from what we call "intellect," *metis* combines resourcefulness with foresight, experience with flair and, sometimes, a bit of cunning. Thus, Athena is credited as the goddess of inventions: she gave humanity the bridle, plow, and yoke; taught the arts of shipbuilding, navigation, goldsmithing, and shoemaking; invented numbers and the flute; and taught women the domestic arts of cooking, spinning, and weaving. Even in sacred ritual, Athena's contributions to civilization were preeminent;

at the Panathenaea, her yearly festival, the *peplos*, a costly garment woven and embroidered by Athenian maidens of the highest rank, was carried to the goddess's temple, the Parthenon, on a great ship on wheels. Through musical competitions and horse racing, the participants showed off their *metis* in Athena's honor.

Athena is the guardian we call on for the discipline and the strategies necessary to make our dreams reality. She can help us understand that, indeed, "Necessity is the mother of invention" and that sometimes the best way to get something done is to combine intuition with a down-to-earth practicality. After all, this goddess devised the Trojan horse, an emblem of craft as well as cunning strategy—the enormous wooden horse presented by the Greeks as a supposed gift to Troy hid enemy Greek soldiers within. Her sacred animal is the owl, which can see and hunt in darkness—symbolic of intuition harnessed to strategic purpose. In that sense, Athena is the guardian of blueprints and plans who can help us find the best way to make something happen—whether taking a step up the corporate ladder, starting a business, remodeling the kitchen, or putting enough money aside for a college fund. You can help strengthen your own capacity for discipline by taking a goal-oriented course or by teaching yourself a skill—it could be knitting, refinishing furniture, or learning a foreign language—as long as you have a specific goal, not just "enrichment" in mind. Other disciplines—such as yoga—will also put more of Athena's special kind of smarts into your life. When calling on Athena, make an effort to bring more order and discipline into your life; for the moment at least, going with the flow won't help you arrive at your chosen destination. Buy yourself a planner, make a schedule, and keep track of your progress. Make sure you leave yourself enough time to finish what you need to do or to arrive at an appointment on time. Set specific goals for yourself.

Sit down and spend time analyzing and visualizing the end result you wish to achieve. Make a list of "first steps"—the information and knowledge you'll need in order to move toward your goal. If it's a promotion you want, approach it tactically. Who has been promoted recently and why? Think about what management values in its employees and ask yourself if your work history reflects those qualities. If it's the kitchen you're remodeling, research your choices. Make sure you know which questions to ask before you start looking for answers. Be practical—Athena isn't the guardian of pipe dreams and has little patience for those whose mantra includes the words "I don't know." Supplant free association with dis-ciplined thought, and proceed in an orderly fashion while keeping your goal in mind.

The martial Athena isn't the guardian to call on for all things; she lacks domesticity, and her cool gaze can detract from the gentle beauties of day-to-day life. But she can help us look long and hard when we need to, without hardening our hearts.

Flexibility
The Bird

We now know what the ancients didn't: these glorious creatures of earth and sky were most probably the evolutionary offspring of the long-vanished dinosaurs, a testament to their flexibility and endurance. But in many cultures, birds in all their variety were especially holy. Specific symbolism was attached to each in kind, among them the eagle and the wren, the dove and the nightingale, the owl and the swan, the peacock and the swallow. In the West, the mythical phoenix was said to rise up from the ashes of the fire that consumed it, making it a potent emblem of immortality. In China, the mythical *feng-huang* was also immortal, combining yin and yang, and thus symbolizing total harmony.

The bird's ability to soar into the skies denotes freedom and flexibility, as well as symbolizes the human desire to break free of the constraints of earth and gravity, the flight of the soul, and the imagination. In many cultures, the soul is pictured as a bird. As a traveler between the two planes of here and there, earth and sky, the bird is also a divine messenger; the Roman augurs studied flight patterns to interpret divine will, while the birds of the Welsh goddess Rhiannon blurred the line between life and death. It was said that the sweetness of birdsong could both awaken the dead and put the living to eternal sleep.

As a traveler between the mundane and the spiritual, the place of reality and of dreams, the bird can show us how to let go of our either/or thinking, and can help us become intellectually, psychologically, and emotionally flexible. By encouraging us to think about links and connections, rather than oppositions, she helps us embrace the power of inclusiveness. By following her example, we can relinquish obdurate thoughts and old patterns that limit our vision, and let our minds and spirits take flight. She lifts our wings when we've become too earthbound—too mired in the here and now—and when we have stopped dreaming. Because Bird perches both on the ground and in the highest branches, hers is the wisdom of perspective; she knows that there is rarely only one way of seeing and that much depends on the height and distance from which we see.

To bring Bird into your life, feed your soul and let new ideas invigorate your discourse and thought. Use your journal to explore new connections and points of view.

Initiate discussions with different friends and let yourself truly listen to them. There is much to learn. Take a course that incorporates group discussion, or join a reading group, to open your mind.

You may wish to adopt a specific bird as your specific spirit guide. Each bird symbolizes a different quality and has a unique lesson to teach, helping us develop more flexible responses and behaviors.

Dove: In ancient times, the dove was associated with both sexuality and physical joy; in the Christian tradition, she came to symbolize peace, love, and purity, which are her primary meanings today. She calls forth our gentler, more understanding side, and is a guardian of conciliation, not strong action.

Eagle: The emblem of speed, power, and majesty in every culture, Eagle can be a special guardian when we feel weak, inadequate, or inflexible. She can help restore our vision if we have become caught up in petty details or we can't see the proverbial forest for the trees; her ability to soar to great heights can inspire us to be not so single-minded. The eagle is also a solar symbol and the guardian of priests, seers, and shamans the world over, but especially among the Native Americans. Her immense spiritual power encourages us to rise above the ordinary and mundane.

Nightingale: Perhaps the most eloquent of the songbirds, she is often associated with love, both its passions and its loss; she is the inspiration of poets and dreamers. Call upon the nightingale for inspiration and release the part of you that is superorganized and insistent on having everything "just so." She'll help you kick off your shoes and walk barefoot through a meadow.

Owl: Guardian of wisdom and learning, as well as the night, she guides us to discover new philosophies and, with the keenness of her eyesight, lets us gain perspective on where we've been. Owl can also provide a corrective for the overexuberant personality that has confused excess with energy.

Peacock: While vanity is now most frequently associated with this noble bird—though only the male is flamboyant—Peacock has a long sacral history. The bird of the Greek goddess Hera and the Roman Juno, the peacock was an emblem of the soul and spiritual power. Similarly, in Hinduism, she was an attribute of the goddess of wisdom, Sarasvati, while in Buddhism, the peacock epitomized renouncing worldly attachment. Call upon Peacock to encourage flexible spiritual growth; as a solar emblem, it she brings forth spiritual illumination.

Swallow: Messenger of spring, she is the perfect guardian when we want our newfound flexibility to yield new growth in our lives. In China, she was the harbinger of promise and prosperity, and thought to encompass both yin and yang, since she took the form of a shell or bivalve in winter—the season of yin—and emerged in her bird shape during summer, the season of yang.

Swan: Possessed of a complex history, she is associated with love, poetry, and especially transformation; she was sacred to the Greek goddess of love, Aphrodite, as well as to the god of poetry, music, and prophesy, Apollo. The Celts associated her with the otherworld and believed that spirits often took the shape of swans when they returned to earth, traveling in pairs linked by a golden or silver chain. Swan can teach us to be flexible in love and to believe in the power of transformation. She helps us embrace differences in those we love as well.

Wren: Small and unassuming—perching almost unseen among the branches of the tree—she reminds us that loud and large aren't always the best response to every situation in life. She was associated with prophesy by the Celts and with simplicity and happiness among the Native Americans. As a guardian, she teaches us to turn down the volume.

Generosity
Lakshmi

Who better to help us achieve generosity of spirit and action than the Hindu goddess Lakshmi, who assures prosperity and abundance? She was, as scholar Heinrich Zimmer detailed, originally an earth goddess closely connected to India's agrarian culture, but over time, she came to symbolize both material and spiritual prosperity. She represents an active principle in the universe—her name in Sanskrit means "goal" or "aim"—and the symbols attached to this goddess point to the connection, not the conflict, between the spiritual and material worlds.

She is often pictured with large breasts, signifying her maternal nature, and accompanied by two elephants whose raised trunks shower her with life-giving water. The elephants convey myriad meanings: emblems of fertility as well as stability (the universe was thought to rest on the backs of elephants), they also stand for kingship, power, and the renown associated with worldly wealth. By sprinkling Lakshmi, they demonstrate that wealth and prosperity must be shared, not selfishly hoarded. Lakshmi is often pictured showering gold coins with one hand, blessings with another; her two sets of arms—those in front signifying acts in the material world, those in back tending to the spiritual world—underscore the connection between the two realms.

Many of Lakshmi's honorifics specifically tie her to the lotus; she is praised variously as "Lotus-Born," "Standing on a Lotus," "Abounding in Lotuses," or "Garlanded with Lotuses." She is "Lotus-Colored," "Lotus-Eyed," "Lotus-Thighed." The lotus symbolizes the spirit or spiritual fulfillment. Rising out of the darkness of the waters to bloom in the sunlight, its emergence signals the triumph of spirit over matter. Understand the lotus as a symbol of the potential within us, the budded stem that rises out of the small, tight places in our soul and, under Lakshmi's tutelage, flowers into generous acts among family, friends, and community members.

To become truly generous, we must first perceive ourselves as prosperous, possessed of gifts we can share with the world. It's one thing to calculate how much money is in the bank and quite another to take stock of the things that enrich the spirit. Invite Lakshmi into your life by counting your blessings, both spiritual and material; make a list of all the gifts life has given you each day. Remember the small things as well as the large ones. Has someone helped you, unasked? Did kind words smooth a rough day? At week's end, think about the ways you have or haven't reciprocated those blessings. Generosity can take many forms. If you are vital and healthy, share your energy with someone who isn't. If you've been blessed with a patient and caring partner or friend, become a good listener for someone who finds herself alone and unheard. If you have a gift or talent, teach it to someone else—passing the riches of pleasure or attainment along. There are many in our society, young and old, who can benefit.

Awareness of the abundance in our lives encourages the growth of our own generosity. Incorporate a blessing bowl ceremony at mealtimes to help each member of your family, no matter how young, become more generous in act and spirit. Have each person write down a single "gift" received during the day—anything that made the day happier, easier, more meaningful or fulfilling—on a folded piece of paper and place it in the blessing bowl. At the end of the week, open up all the slips and "recount" them by reading them aloud. Then have everyone write down a blessing he or she wishes someone else to receive, and spend time talking about how to manifest these blessings in the spirit of Lakshmi, goddess of abundance.

Groundedness
Gaia

S he is the oldest of the Greek goddesses, Mother Earth, the descendant of the Great Goddess whose many names have been lost. Traces remain of her power and magnificence, bearing witness to the fact that long before the Greeks lifted their eyes skyward to Zeus's dominion, they honored the primal mother who gave birth to and contained all of nature within her body; in the Homeric Hymn, she is praised as "mother of all, foundation of all."

We turn to Gaia when flights of fancy have become the norm, when the winds of change spin us around like a whirligig. She provides sure footing when we're in danger of stumbling. She can help us hear our inner voice when noise drowns it out; bring us back when we wander into dangerous places or engage in risky behaviors; encourage us to heal the breach when we isolate ourselves and lose connection to the people and activities that give life meaning. She is there when the fast pace of life overtakes our spirits, and leaves us with nothing but a marked-up calendar and a vague memory of how we spent our time.

There is much you can do to let Gaia into your life. Honor the diurnal rhythms so that you wake up refreshed. Use the resources of Mother Earth consciously, thoughtfully, and thankfully; remind yourself that the food that fuels you is her gift. Grow conscious of the products and behaviors that squander, waste, or pollute Earth's treasures. Restore your sense of harmony with nature's rhythms by eating only the fruits and vegetables in season where you live; by cutting your ties to the natural course of the harvest, you may add to your sense of being unmoored.

Take a long walk every day, as far into nature as you can manage; if you live in a city, head for a park. Breathe deep and let the earth begin to heal you. Gaia teaches in every season: in winter, the lesson of unseen growth and rebirth; in spring, the miracle of new beginnings and emergence; in summer, the glory of long-awaited harvest; in fall, the necessary rest that precedes new growth. By observing the larger rhythms of nature, you can begin to understand where you are in your own personal cycle of life—is the cycle emergent, in flower, or at rest?—and find a surer footing. Honor the Earth Mother by gardening outdoors or tending houseplants indoors.

Begin to build a calm center within by meditating every day. In many traditions, stones are Earth's children, and using minerals and gemstones as a part of meditation will help connect you to Gaia's healing. You can choose stones by color if you like—green for rebirth, blue for intelligence and clarity, for example—or use minerals that have traditional healing associations, such as amethyst (calm and sobriety), crystal quartz (clarity), hematite (rebirth), or carnelian (tranquility). In the Native American Southwestern tradition, turquoise was Earth's holy stone.

Use your journal to plan and think things through so that whatever dreams and flights of fancy have sent you tumbling off balance can either be discarded or translated into reality. If you decide to hang on to those dreams, work on building secure foundations for them. Gaia will help you keep your feet on terra firma.

Remember that, as Mother Nature, Gaia is spirit incarnate in the clouds, trees, rocks, and creatures on our blue planet. You are part of her eternal cycle.

Independence
Epona

I n the mind's eye, she is never solitary, always accompanied by horses or in the midst of them. Sometimes, she rides sidesaddle without reins, a foal beside her; to ride the horse astride would give her mastery, but she prefers her equine companion to be as independent as she is. Ancient images confirm that Epona and her horses are a company of equals: they feed from her hand; she reclines on a mare's back; a foal sleeps beneath the mare at Epona's feet. A Celtic goddess, Epona was revered by the fierce Roman cavalry as a protector who nourished horses and kept them free from injury; they may have discovered her wisdom when they conquered Gaul, and Epona was the only Celtic deity they brought back to Rome.

Paradoxically, she remains wholly feminine in nature despite her link to the horse, emblem of male vitality and power. She is a goddess of plenty, and the cornucopia and the sheaf of grain are among her attributes. The waters and springs that lie hidden from view deep in the earth are connected to her, connoting fertility, healing, and inspiration. Of course, the horse and the waters are symbolically connected as well. Pegasus, the winged horse of the Greeks, created the spring of Hippocrene, sacred to the Muses, when he stamped his hoof. In fact, the world over, mythical and real horses alike were thought to be able to find and release hidden springs and wells.

Epona is the guardian of our independence, the mythic foremother to the girl who longs to roam freely with wild horses, hair streaming out behind her in the wind. She is the repository of many girlhood dreams of riders and horses, of Black Beauty, Flicka, and Pie; of girls growing strong and proud. She is the mirror to the part of us that loves the independent spirit of the cowgirl and the feistiness of all those women who are determined to step out boldly and go where no woman has gone before.

Little is preserved of Epona's sacred story. We know that Romans honored her by hanging garlands in their horses' stalls. It may be that the Great White Horse of Uffington in England—its almost four-hundred-foot equine outline etched into the chalky hill and visible only from a great height—was once dedicated to her. But we can catch glimpses of her in the varied and universal symbolism of her companion, the horse. Closely associated with Earth's fruition and the underworld (the Greek

Demeter was sometimes portrayed as horse headed), this powerful animal was also identified with the moon and, later, with the sun. While the stallion symbolizes the power of fertility and instinct, the mare is closely associated with the Earth Mother herself; Epona is a protector of the horse in both its male and female aspects.

Epona is the guardian of our own vital energy. She inspires us to honor our individuality, our unique thoughts and feelings. She supports the part of us that can spend time alone without feeling lonely or abandoned; her cowgirl wisdom reminds us to speak our minds when we need to and not to let anyone do our thinking for us. She encourages our self-reliance, even though, as a nurturer and Earth Mother, she also stands for emotional connection. As a healer, she helps us rid ourselves of unhealthy and needy dependencies that get in the way of true relationships.

Invite the spirit of this guardian into your life by reading books by or about strong, independent women who have helped shape the world we live in. Anne Morrow Lindbergh's *Gift from the Sea* exquisitely renders a woman's balancing act between her own need for independence and the needs of those dependent upon her. Involve yourself in activities that bolster girls' and women's sense of themselves as independent and strong.

Use your journal to explore what's holding you back from healthy independence. If you habitually criticize yourself, spend some time focusing on your strengths, instead of your weaknesses. Work on acknowledging your own needs and make time and space for them. Every woman, as Virginia Woolf observed, needs "a room of her own." Remind yourself that an independent spirit actually facilitates stronger connections and commitments.

And see yourself as a bold, empowered traveler along the path of life with a horse by your side.

Ingenuity
Ariadne

For matters great and small—the balancing acts of all of our lives—we call upon Ariadne to help us find a hidden talent when we're confronted by a challenge. This quality provides the remedy when our other efforts to resolve or change a situation have fallen short. Ingenuity helps us find a new route when the road is closed, mend a bad breach with perfectly chosen words, or tape up a hem with whatever sticky is at hand. It is what inspires us to make lemonade when life hands us a truckload of lemons.

Begin by remembering that the words *ingenuity* and *ingenious* have the words *spirit* or *guardian* buried within them. *Ingenious* and *genius* have shared Latin roots, and what we call cleverness or ingeniousness, the Romans credited to the specific genius or spirit who presided over every individual's birth. *Ingeniousness* (or, as the Romans had it, *ingenium*) was innate—something you were born with, provided by your resident spirit.

Keeping this in mind, we turn to the Greek Ariadne.

Her story tells us that the simplest of resources can become the greatest of tools when we call upon our ingeniousness—our innate spirit—to solve the problem at hand. Ariadne teaches us not to look high or far to find a solution but to look simply and clearly.

Most often, what we need is no more than the thread of wisdom we already possess.

Ariadne was the daughter of Minos, the legendary king of Crete, and his wife Pasiphaë, whose connection to lunar wisdom is indicated by her name, which means "all shining." Minos had disobeyed the wishes of Poseidon, the mighty god of the oceans, and in punishment, Poseidon caused Pasiphaë to fall in love with a bull. Pasiphaë then gave birth to a monster, the Minotaur—half man, half beast—who was imprisoned in an impenetrable labyrinth. Each year, the best of Athenian youth was sacrificed to satisfy the monster's hungers. Ariadne fell in love with the hero Theseus whose task was to kill the Minotaur—in the labyrinth from which no one had ever emerged alive.

Although myth presents her as mortal, Ariadne may well have been a moon goddess like her mother, for her name means "all holy." The wisdom she possessed was as simple and clear as the reflected light of the moon in the night: she gave Theseus no more than a humble thread to unwind as he made his way through the maze to its center and to guide him out again while she held its end fast in her hand. Ariadne's ingenuity permitted Theseus to emerge from the labyrinth intact, to emerge from darkness into light, as a victor and hero.

In the same way, our small ingenuities—the special ways we wrap gifts, make an impromptu dinner feel like a party, or comfort a crying child—permit everyday beauties and joys to emerge fully for ourselves and those around us. This same thread of ingenuity allows us to navigate larger crises or problems with resourcefulness and clarity.

Ariadne teaches us that true ingenuity lies deep within our spirit, a ray of moonlight temporarily hidden away from view. She reminds us to look for the simple solution first and foremost, and to trust our instincts when we think we have found an answer. Her wisdom is lunar—intuitive, deep, and stirring. We need to rid ourselves of distraction so that we can enter the maze we need to confront and allow our inner thread to guide us out.

Choose a bit of colored string, cord, yarn, or ribbon symbolic of the thread within. Choose any color except black. Among those you may want to consider are white, color of the new moon; purple, signifying deliberate action; or red, for energy and strength. You can keep the string loose and unknotted in your pocket or purse, or tie it around your wrist in a circle of completion. Remember that the string can keep you tethered when you feel you are in danger of drifting away from what needs to be done. It is also a reminder that the most complicated of weavings begins with a single thread. Ariadne's wisdom can lead us into the future.

Try to visualize the answer you already possess but cannot access. Look in a mirror and imagine Ariadne's knowledge within you. Look past the surface—past the details of eyes, skin, hair—and focus on the self within. Let your inner spirit—the repository of all the many threads of imagination, creativity, and resourcefulness unique to you—rise to the surface. In your journal, write about the ways in which you've dealt with challenges in the past, and work on recognizing their common threads. Look at these links closely, and your ingenuity will come forth.

Intellect
Themis

The Greek goddess of justice, Themis symbolized order, harmony, and truth; she was pictured with a cornucopia in one hand, signifying the gifts and blessings of justice, and a pair of scales in the other. Dispassionate and unswerving, she is wisdom born of reason and intellect; her scales symbolize her deliberate and thoughtful understanding. She represents moderation, careful parsing, and clarity of thought—the jurist and the scholar both "weigh" facts and statements—and provides a balance to responses shaped primarily by emotion or pure intuition.

Themis is there when we need to think a situation through, when we need to study hard and learn something thoroughly, when we need to weigh the alternatives open to us by using facts and figures, when we need to expand our intellectual understanding of people and situations. Importantly, the Greeks did not consider her particular kind of intelligence—the impartial weighing of the facts, which reflected both the divine and moral orders—to be a repudiation of other kinds of wisdom, such as the prophetic. In fact, in one tradition, the oracle at Delphi, which had originally belonged to Gaia, became sacred to Themis before it was taken over by Apollo. Reason, Themis reminds us, is not the domain of men alone; even we daughters of the moon and heiresses of intuitive gifts can claim it as our own without feeling that it is inimical to our nature.

Themis is the guardian of all endeavors that yield new patterns of thought; she is the patron of study, research, and education, whether for edification or advancement. She provides balance to the more creative, less structured side of intellectual endeavor and encourages us to lay a solid foundation of knowledge and information.

Order and logic are paramount to Themis, since what is scattered or piled can't be weighed and assessed. Make sure that external disorganization—piled-up papers, sloppy files, messy closets, and disorganized schedules—aren't getting in the way of true learning.

Stimulate your intellect by choosing how to spend your downtime. If you're in the car a lot, turn on a public radio station or pop in a spoken-word cassette. Read the newspaper every morning—don't let television force-feed you the facts—and, when you are watching television, pick a program that will teach you something new. Join a reading group to improve your analytical skills and powers of persuasion. Take an adult education course that will really challenge you. Use the Internet as a research tool to expand your knowledge.

Themis reminds us that intellectual growth is a part of spiritual growth and that education is a lifelong process. Take inspiration from the women who embarked on new intellectual and creative journeys late in life, such as Julia Child, who published her first cookbook at the age of fifty-nine, or Grandma Moses, who started painting in her seventies.

Intention
Isis

She was the most revered of the Egyptian goddesses. Called "Isis of a Thousand Names" because she had so many aspects and associations, she was venerated for thousands of years, up through Roman times. She was always portrayed in human form, identified either by the hieroglyphic of her name ("throne") or the horns of the cow on her head. She was wife, mother, and supporter of law, the arts, and the legitimacy of kings. Supremely intelligent and always purposeful, she became a goddess by virtue of her own drive. An ancient story recounts how she contrived to find the magic-filled name of the sun god Re, which he had confided in no one. Isis fashioned a snake out of Re's spittle mixed with earth, and this snake bit the god. Overcome by agony and convinced of his impending death, Re called upon Isis to help him as a last resort. She answered that only the revelation of his true name would cure him. Though Re tried to trick Isis with other names, she persisted; once he revealed his name to her, she became a goddess.

Her stories reveal her underlying humanity, which may explain why she was so beloved—a goddess with a woman's heart and purpose. She is the guardian of intention and her sphere is love, family, and relationship. We can turn to Isis when we need help honoring our intention pertaining to matters of the heart and soul. She represents devotion and love made manifest in actions.

While there are many variations of her sacred story, each contains similar elements. Isis was married to her brother Osiris, whom she dearly loved, and who had brought civilization, the arts, and knowledge into the world. But their brother Seth was jealous of Osiris's accomplishments and fashioned a beautifully made chest of rare woods. He tricked Osiris into lying in the chest and then, with a host of conspirators, nailed it shut. Seth flung the chest into the Nile, where it floated out to sea. Left widowed and childless, Isis was devastated. Cutting her hair and rending her clothes, she mourned Osiris deeply and committed herself to finding the chest so that she could give her husband a proper burial. She searched alone for months on end, until she finally found the chest in Byblos. Among the variants of the story is one in which Isis opened the chest and turned herself into a hawk; enfolding her husband's body, she beat her wings furiously so that the air became the breath of eternal life. Osiris was momentarily revived, and she conceived their son Horus. She then took the chest home and, intending to bury it, set it among the reeds of the Nile. But Seth came upon it first, and this time, he tore Osiris's body into fourteen pieces, which he scattered all over the land. Yet again, Isis went in search of her husband's body, gathering up each piece as she found it. In the end, she found all the pieces save one—his penis, which had been swallowed by a fish or crab. Once more, she restored him to wholeness—fashioning a new organ—so that he could be buried and enjoy eternal life in the underworld.

Isis's journeys are arduous and painful—reminding us that following the path of intention and true love may not always be quick or easy. She achieves her goal but can't escape pain and suffering; while she restores Osiris to life in the underworld and bears their child, he is not returned to her in this world. Literally and metaphorically, true redress and restoration elude her—reminding us that our intentions should not be tempered by results that differ from those we sought and expected. Her dedication to her husband and her unwavering purpose, despite hardship and pain, make her a guardian of those intentions that are tried by events beyond our control.

Bring the power of Isis into your life by affirming your intentions each day. Imagine her wings enfolding you and strengthening your resolve. Apply her strength in your own journey.

Use the following affirmation to begin a practice of writing an affirmation each morning and reading it aloud:

> I will focus my energy on my true intentions.
>   I will not be distracted by noise, chatter,
> or setbacks. Patience, commitment, grace, and
> purpose will guide me.

Intuition
Selene

Whether we call her "Selene" or "Luna," as the Greeks and Romans did, or one of the other many names by which she is known the world over matters little; it is always the moon we invoke as the guardian of intuition. In contrast to the rational knowledge symbolized by the sun's bright light, moon wisdom perceives without reasoning, drawing on the truths we have absorbed from dreams and experiences, but which lie below the level of consciousness. Selene's gift is the knowledge based on connections that can't be teased out rationally. The word *intuition* comes from the Latin "to look at," and intuitive perception has a directness like no other; with it, seeing and knowing are condensed into a single moment of illumination.

The powerful myths connecting this changing heavenly body to earthly cycles and to the menstrual cycle of women must themselves have been intuitively grasped. In the waxing, waning, disappearance, and reemergence of the moon, humans saw a pattern analogous to the cycles of nature: a story of life, death, and rebirth; an echo of the cycles of the female body. Increase—growth in vegetation, animals, humans—was thought to come from the light of the moon, not the sun; the moon goddess was also the keeper of certain kinds of knowledge, such as time and measurement.

The power this ancient moon mythos once held can be glimpsed by the force with which succeeding patriarchal myths supplanted it. The moon became a symbol of mutability; the terms *lunatic*, *lunacy*, *mooning* (acting listless or aimless), *moon madness*, *moonstruck*, and even *moonshine* (without substance) testify to the goddess's dethronement. Intuition became synonymous with a "guess" or a "hunch," the inferior opposite of the sun's pure light of reason.

But lunar knowledge can be reclaimed as we acknowledge the power and integrity of our changing bodies. We can honor the heightened awareness and sensitivity many of us experience during our menstrual cycles or their waning.

Keep a journal and bring Selene's power into your life. Record your dreams and flashes of insight. You are a repository of information and knowledge that can be applied fruitfully in your life. Learn to trust your instincts and intuition; pay attention to those flashes of insight that flutter in your belly, that sense of déjà vu.

Opening ourselves to the power of images and symbols in art and literature can help strengthen the connections on which intuition depends. Try writing poetry or painting, or appreciate the work of others: read poetry, visit a museum, or take an art book out of the library. The paintings of Henri Rousseau or Vincent Van Gogh may be a good place to start. Be aware that spending hours in front of a television or computer will only decrease your own moon goddess power.

Finally, take a walk in the moonlight and try to recover that sense of awe and wonder humans once felt when they looked up to see the great goddess who lit the way in the dark of night.

Joy
The Three Graces

The Greeks called them the *Charites,* or *Charis,* from the word *chairein* ("to rejoice"), while the Romans named them *Gratiae,* or Graces. Friends to the Muses, the goddesses of literature and art, the Graces were often pictured in the company of Aphrodite, the goddess of love—reminders that the arts confer happiness and that love and joy are often intertwined. They were three: Aglaia ("brightness"), euphrosyne ("joyfulness"), and Thalia ("bloom" or "blossoming one").

They were worshipped in Boetia in Greece as unhewn stones fallen from the sky, perhaps as a reminder that joy is indeed a gift of the heavens, and suggesting, as does their triple nature, that they were once connected to the all-giving Earth Goddess. They were feted and invoked with music, dance, and food. Their attributes were musical instruments, the myrtle, and the rose—all strongly associated with love in its physical and mystical aspects. Originally pictured as beautiful young women either holding hands or embracing each other, in time they came to be portrayed with their nude bodies intertwined, one seen from the front and two from behind—embodying grace, loveliness, charm, and, above all, the sweetness of life and womanhood.

We call upon the Graces when our capacity to feel joy seems somehow diminished: when we've gotten too self-involved, when we're worn down by stress, or when we find ourselves in an unhappy transition from one stage of life to another. The Graces can help us when we've suffered a loss or setback.

Their connection to Aphrodite, the goddess of love, is revealing, though we need to bear in mind that Aphrodite's sphere transcends that of romantic or sexual love. The goddess was born of the union of Heaven and Sea and emerged from the sea foam, suggesting that love encompasses all natural connections among many things, both animate and inanimate, belonging to the earth and sky, not only the intimate bond between two individuals. The Graces attend Aphrodite in this transcendent aspect. Thus the Graces protect that aspect of us that awakens when we hear a bird sing or when we are transported by music; they shelter the part of us that is moved by a beautiful sunset, a painting, or the scent of a lily or the loamy earth. They nurture our sensory responses and the diverse ways of feeling joy: the taste of delicious food, the warmth of a smile, the beauty of a butterfly on the wing. The Graces remind us that pleasure isn't an indulgence but an essential part of living; they symbolize all the things in life for which we express gratitude or "grace."

Let the power of the Graces into your life by making sure, first of all, that how you live isn't shutting down your senses. Look at where you live and work not with a decorator's eye but by asking whether you feel happy in your surroundings. Are your senses stimulated? Removing clutter and adding just a few things—an art print or postcards, a brightly colored pillow, a textured throw, fresh flowers or scented candles—will make a difference, even in a windowless office cubicle. Similarly, are you eating on the run or are you sitting down to savor what you eat? Fast food is bad for your body, but arguably even worse for the soul. Given the hurried pace of life, it's no wonder that too many of us feel joyless too much of the time.

Turn off the television, the phone, and the computer, and listen to music instead. Head out to an art gallery, visit a yummy restaurant, or take a walk in the park. Spend an afternoon doing something you love but that you don't always make time for. Let yourself open up to the small joys life offers.

Remember, too, that one way of experiencing joy is to see it reflected in someone else's face. Do something that makes someone else happy—it can be a random act of kindness or a planned good deed. Community service is a way of bringing joy into more than one heart at a time.

With the Graces by our side, we can increase not only the amount of the joy we experience but also our sense of thankfulness for all the happiness, large and small, that life offers. Saying "grace" before a meal or at other times of the day can only bring the Graces into our lives more fully.

Leadership
Joan of Arc

For some six hundred years, her story has inspired painters, poets, novelists, dramatists, filmmakers, and countless numbers of young girls and women—the slip of a peasant girl astride a black charger, her hair cropped like a man's, dressed in a knight's coat of mail, an ancient sword in one hand and a white standard embroidered with lilies in the other, leading her troops to victory. Her vision—informed by divine voices—was nothing less than to deliver her fifteenth-century France from its English conquerors and to transform history. Joan of Arc—*La Pucelle,* or "the maiden," as she called herself—was probably only nineteen years old when she was burned at the stake for two heresies: she refused to deny the existence and divine provenance of her "voices" and to renounce masculine attire. So few physical details remain about the young woman she was—not even a single contemporary portrait survives—that, over the centuries, her story has been a partly filled canvas with room for the individual imagination to add the finishing touches.

Sometime between 1410 and 1412, Joan was born in the village of Domrémy, the daughter of a peasant proprietor. Even though her parents were comparatively well off, she never learned to read or write. Her mother schooled her in the scriptures as well as in the womanly arts of sewing and spinning. In fact, at her trial in Rouen, when she was described by her inquisitors as a "shepherd girl," she objected, saying that no woman in Rouen could rival her skill with the needle and wheel, probably to assert that she had the higher status of a "gentlewoman." But, at the age of sixteen, she refused the man her parents had chosen to be her husband and left home to seek her destiny. In the context of her time, it was an extraordinary gesture of independence and disobedience that defied both convention and expectation—and the first of many. She very deliberately stayed a virgin—hence *La Pucelle*—which, in addition to her spiritual purity, indicated her freedom from male dominion and the social realities of the times.

Her story remains compelling, perhaps because, as biographer Marina Warner notes, she belonged to the "sphere of action" and was a woman "renowned for doing something on her own, not by birthright." She was singular, and would have been even if there weren't so few female heroines bequeathed to us by history. There are so many aspects of Joan that capture the imagination and heart: the tenacity of her vision; her bravery and willingness to stand alone; the way she subverted social norms by assuming masculine looks and roles; her rejection of convention and wifely subjugation; her dedication and confidence; and finally her martyrdom. And then there is the matter of her visions. She believed herself to be divinely inspired to be sure, but it was only under pressure at the trial that she gave the voices names and shapes. Were they externalizations of her own imagination, which, under fire, she explained by reference to the stories of angels and saints she'd been told as a child? It matters little if we understand her visions as literal or metaphorical; they gave her the power to do and act. (The Catholic Church affirmed those visions when they made her a saint in 1920.)

Joan of Arc's story resonates even today, when women wear pants and cut their hair to suit themselves, and young girls swing upside down from jungle gyms and dream of becoming president. Much has changed in the centuries since Joan lived. Call upon Joan when you feel conflicted about needing or wanting to assume a position of leadership. Leadership involves visibility and responsibility, which can be both a gift and a bane; expect that, as a leader, you will be scrutinized more carefully and criticized more openly. Joan reminds us that there are risks in becoming a leader. Remember that leaders (and bosses) have to hire and fire; the armor Joan wore into battle was real, but you will need some armor of your own when assuming a position of leadership. To lead effectively, you must nourish and trust your own visions of the future; the example of Joan of Arc can help you there as well.

Finally, keep Joan's story by your side when cultural ambivalence about women in power begins to get you down. Take on some of the strength and conviction of that eighteen-year-old foremother who rode her horse with her banner held high; do your best to lead wisely and well.

Productivity
The Bee

For millennia, the bee has been inseparable from the complex symbolism of the honey and the honeycomb she produces. Honey stands for the sweetness and purity of life and is associated with poetry, eloquence, and expression of the spirit. From ancient times onward, poets and philosophers were said to have been fed with honey, their lips sweetened with its essence. Like ambrosia, honey is the food of the gods, and the bee was a symbol of the spark of divine intelligence; in ancient Egypt, the bee was born from the sun god Re's tears. Because honey needs neither preparation nor cooking to be eaten, it was a primal, sacral food in many cultures. Honey was used to anoint acolytes in the initiation rites of ancient Greece and was associated with the sweetness of nirvana in Hinduism. The priestesses of the Greek goddess of earth, Demeter, were called *Melissae,* or "bees," as were those of Cybele; the moon, according to Porphyry, was also sometimes addressed as "Bee," or Melissa. Since the moon was perceived as a feminine agent of generation and regeneration, it isn't surprising that the bee belonged to her.

One of the first known preservatives, honey was used to embalm the dead in ancient Egypt and thus is associated with rebirth as well as magic. Fermented honey, or mead, was used in ecstatic rituals both in Minoan civilization and among the Celts. And there is the honeycomb—a symbol of the earth, because it holds the riches of honey, and of the hidden interconnectedness of all things, because of its interior cellular design. It is no wonder that the bee, her honey, and her honeycomb were associated with the divine feminine, long before they were incorporated into the symbolism of Judeo-Christian traditions.

And then there is the bee herself—of the earth, yet winged and thus of the sky. Honey also connects to both the earth and sky—the bee sips nectar from the earthbound flower and then flies upward—and so the bee symbolizes both the material and the spiritual worlds. The activity and productivity of the bee—the buzzing hive and the rapid flapping of her wings—make her emblematic of the life force, vitality, and the connection between the individual and the community. Finally, the bee stands for illumination, in part because of the purity of her wax and the bright flame it yields.

Bee inspires us when we feel listless and lackluster at work or when we feel we've worked hard and come away with nothing. She reminds us that life is sweet—and that work produces great riches, material and spiritual.

As a guardian, Bee not only teaches us to be productive by example—she is as hardworking and diligent as the homilies portray her—but also encourages us to explore why we aren't as inventive or energetic as we want to be. She has us ask ourselves whether the paths we follow—the work we do, the relationships we have, the way we spend our time—produce what we want and need. She prods us to question whether our needs are being met when we come home from work, day after day, exhausted and depressed. She reminds us that we achieve more when we work in the company of others equally committed and diligent. Because she represents both the material and the spiritual, Bee has us look at both our bank accounts and the feeding of our souls. As a guardian of tasks and goals—the bee stores away more honey than she needs in anticipation of the cold months ahead—she can help us discern the career paths and relationships that no longer serve the needs of the present and the future.

Surround yourself with beeswax candles to bring this guardian's special gifts into your life and let them shed light on your situation. Ask yourself what is holding you back from being more productive. Open yourself to imagining work that would leave you more fulfilled and offer sweeter rewards.

With Bee by your side, dreaming takes on another aspect. As Emily Dickinson wrote:

> To make a prairie it takes a clover and one bee,
> One clover, and a bee,
> And revery.
> The revery alone will do,
> If bees are few.

Self-Esteem
The Amazon

Fierce and independent, she is the warrior queen to whom we turn when we feel under siege and need to protect the very core of the self. She can help us recognize the people and situations that make us feel insecure about our abilities, unsure of our opinions, uncomfortable in our skins—and lends us her strength to move away from them. She helps us throw off the cloak of self-doubt and lets us stand tall, head high and body straight. Her half-moon shield, the bow in her hand, and her quiver full of arrows represent the inner wisdom, passions, and ideas that make us strong. She can help awaken our boldest spirit so that we can see the beautiful, strong, and capable Amazon woman within each and every one of us. She is the necessary antidote to a culture in which standards and ideals pertaining to women are contradictory and often impossible to meet. Many of us, beginning in girlhood, have trouble laying claim to feelings of self-worth and struggle with self-doubt even in the wake of success.

Reclaiming the Amazon as our guardian is not altogether different from reclaiming our sense of self, since the story of the woman warrior was told by those who equated female strength with man hating. The Greek historian Herodotus described the Amazons in detail, though he admitted he'd never seen one. Both Greek history and legend attest to the matriarchal Amazon tribes, a nation of warrior women, universally feared for their prowess and strength, who permitted no men or boys to live among them; it was said that once a year the Amazons would sleep with the men of a neighboring tribe, the Gargareans, simply to continue their lineage. Accounts varied as to whether male children born of these unions were returned to their fathers or killed. Girls, on the other hand, were trained in agricultural pursuits, hunting, and the arts of war.

The tribe's name, it was thought, derived from *a mazon,* or "without breast," based on the belief that the Amazons burned or cut off their right breasts so that they could use their bows more freely, a notion that underscored their image as "unnatural" women. But in works of art, they were always depicted as beautiful, full-breasted women, and were often shown wearing thin, short dresses (so they could run and ride freely) like those seen in sculptures and friezes of Artemis the huntress; later works of art show them wearing tight trouser-like garments. It seems more likely that their name meant, as Robert Graves suggested, "many-breasted" (just as Artemis of Ephesus was shown having many breasts) or derived from the Circassian word for "moon," perhaps because they were dedicated to an Asiatic moon goddess similar to the Greek Artemis or the Roman Diana. It has long been suggested that the stories of the Amazon were rooted in tales of women warriors on horseback as reported by travelers to places beyond the Greek territories. Recent archaeological finds by Dr. Jeannine Davis-Kimball, reported in her book *Warrior Women*, suggest that this may indeed be possible.

Call upon the Amazon to bolster your sense of self when it has been eroded by too much negativism or not enough support. Remember that the warrior women Davis-Kimball discovered do not appear to have been aggressive conquerors but simply women who were capable of defending what was theirs when necessary. Amazon wisdom does not encompass territorial aggression or winning for the sake of winning, nor does it imply that "armoring" the self is either useful or beneficial. See her instead as a warrior princess whom we can call on instead of the proverbial "knight in shining armor" to validate our self-esteem. It is the Amazon within who allows us to see past the surface image when we look in the mirror and to say with confidence, "You are ready to face the world" or, "You can do what you need to." She lets us take in both our gifts and our shortcomings with a single, knowing glance—without focusing on one or the other. She reminds us that nothing on this earth is truly "perfect."

Let Amazon wisdom empower you to separate yourself from those who seem bent on reinforcing your insecurities, or, if estrangement isn't what you want, to discuss your feelings and observations with them openly and honestly. Confrontation can be a mark of health.

Cultivate this guardian by reading books that can strengthen your self-esteem and help you better understand the pressures you face. Among the titles you might find useful are Mary Pipher's *Reviving Ophelia*, an excellent primer on the cultural background of self-esteem issues, and Gloria Steinem's *Revolution from Within*, which details how success and self-doubt can coexist, if uncomfortably, in a single woman.

Spontaneity
Artemis

The "Mistress of the Wild Animals" as well as the supreme huntress—creator and destroyer both—Artemis presides over untamed and unfettered nature. As the goddess of instinct, she helps women and animals manage the throes of childbirth. A virgin goddess, she is undomesticated, belongs to no one, and sets her own rules. A force of nature, she is fully independent. Her wisdom is lunar and intuitive—the counterbalance to the knowledge possessed by her twin brother, Apollo—and in ancient times, she was sometimes identified with the crescent or new moon.

Because Artemis represents elemental nature, we call upon her to balance the aspects of personality that can sometimes confine and limit us: our timidity and hesitation, our fearfulness, our unwillingness to try anything new. Artemis helps us step out beyond the boundaries that have been set for us or that we have, by habit, etched for ourselves. She is the antidote to the fat planner we carry everywhere and to our closet full of neutrals, blacks, and sensible shoes. She lets us nurture the risk-taker, the wild woman, within us—the woman who dreams of traveling to the savannahs of Africa or the sacred precincts of Japan, who longs to become an artist or photographer, or who simply wants to live life with a bit more spontaneity.

Connect with Artemis by taking the phrase "If I only could, I would . . ." and writing down all the ways you can finish the sentence. Look at the dreams and wishes you've set down on the page and think about what really is holding you back from fulfilling them. Don't second-guess yourself; let the first thought be the true thought.

For most of us, a life ruled by this goddess of the wilderness—whose voice was thought to echo with the trills of birdsong, the waterfall's thunder—wouldn't work. But every now and then, there is the right time for Artemis to guide us to do precisely what we want at the moment we want it.

Feed your soul by letting your senses and instincts take over for once. Connect with Artemis by leaving civilization behind for a while and let go of all your practical, worldly concerns. Go out into the countryside—particularly if you live in an urban area—and open up your senses to nature. Listen for the songs of birds and the music of the rustling leaves, follow the meandering path of a brook or stream, feel the heat of the sun on your bare back, pack a picnic basket full of delicious foods so you can savor every bite. Dance under the sun to honor her as the ancients did. Or decide to take a spur-of-the-moment trip to somewhere you've never been; ignore that inner voice that says you don't have time. Instead, listen to the wild woman within—Artemis, of the golden bow and arrows—and go wherever her spirit takes you.

Transformation
The Butterfly

Change is almost always difficult—whether we choose it or it is forced upon us by circumstance. We are all creatures of habit, and the work of transforming the self—whether body or soul—is hard, as is moving from one stage of life to another.

The butterfly can be our teacher and guide. Since ancient times, the extraordinary metamorphosis of the butterfly—from egg to caterpillar to chrysalis to winged beauty—has symbolized transformation, rebirth, and regeneration. Her change from earthbound caterpillar to creature of the air led the Greeks to call her "psyche" or soul; similarly, the Aztecs imagined the butterfly as the last breath of life made manifest, and the butterflies flying over flower-laden fields as the spirits of slain warriors. The Christian tradition amplified older associations by connecting the butterfly to spiritual resurrection through Christ.

On the simplest level, the butterfly symbolizes our desire to rise above the quotidian and the material; she stands for the evolved and confident self we can see in the clearest of dreams. She is an epiphany of the moment when our talents fully unfold, when our best qualities shine forth, when we emerge as the women we wish to be.

Of all the butterflies, perhaps the exquisite monarch serves as the best teacher of the work of transformation. Emergence, Monarch tells us, isn't easy or quick; her new life stage as a butterfly begins with hard effort as she shakes and shudders to slip through the single opening in the pupa. When all of her efforts yield escape from its confines, she must suddenly still herself so her wings, wet and malleable, can dry and gain flexibility. She waits, hanging quietly, for a day or more before she can spread her wings and fly. You need reserves of patience, Monarch teaches, if you dream of changing.

If she is one of the last generation of monarchs born each summer, her life cycle will end with two long journeys—a flight of over two thousand miles from the east coast so she can winter in California or Mexico and then return part of the way back—before she can bring the next generation to life. The journey south lasts over two months as this whisper-light creature contends with wind and weather. She glides part of the way on wind currents to conserve energy, as she needs to flap her wings hundreds of times a minute simply to move forward. Patience, Monarch counsels, is balanced by sheer determination. The journey south and then north again is full of starts and stops; she will feed as she goes, and take shelter from rain, gusts of wind, and predators. Only a single plant, the milkweed, will allow her eggs to become larvae, and she will fly until she finds it. Hold the dream fast and trust in it, Monarch whispers.

So too transforming the self is a journey made up of segments, stages, steps. Sometimes we will need to let go of familiar places, people, ways of looking at life to become the women we dream of being. We may find ourselves taking temporary shelter, as the butterfly does, long before we reach our destination. We do not know how the butterfly finds her way, and for us, too, the journey of transformation will sometimes require that we go forward with nothing but instinct as our guide. We will relearn patience as we wait for the next leg of the journey to make itself known to us. We will gather energy from the power of our dreams, resting our wings as we float on the currents of desires and wishes. The only compass we possess is the one deep inside.

Build an altar honoring your desire to transform yourself and your life. Use images of the butterfly or of the other creatures that symbolize transformation, such as the frog or the skin-shedding snake. Use images and pictures that you associate with your own transformation and dreams, as well as circles (emblems of completion) or spirals (signifying energy) as evidence of your determination. Sit before the altar you've created and let yourself dream of shaking free of the chrysalis and taking wing.

Most of all, be patient with yourself and the process, whether the transformation you seek is physical or spiritual. Sometimes, growth requires us to take a step back before we can move forward.

Relationship

Choice
Trivia

She is, first and foremost, the goddess of the crossroads, that sacred place devoted to destiny and choice; her attribute is the torch, which illuminates the unknown pathway. Her Latin name means "She of the Three Ways," but the Greeks worshipped her as Hecate, "She Who Works from Afar." While Hecate is now most often associated with witchcraft, she was, in fact, a powerful goddess who bestowed all wealth and blessings in life. Because she ruled over all three realms—heaven, earth, and the underworld—she was understood as having a triple aspect. She was sometimes pictured with three faces and always associated with the phases of the moon. The crossroads is universally recognized as a place of revelation and manifestation, marking the boundary between the known and the unknown. In Greece, it was also perceived as the intersection between earth and the underworld, which yields Hecate's association with the souls of the dead, the dogs of hell, and protective spells.

In cultures the world over, offerings were left and

shrines built at the crossroads to propitiate the spirits, to express gratitude for safe passage, and to reassure nervous travelers.

Trivia is the guardian of choice: the moment at which we decide to leave or stay, to commit ourselves further to a given path or to choose another. She presides over all the choices, large and small, that give shape to each individual woman's life. Sometimes, the significance of certain choices is easily grasped—when we choose a career, a mate, or motherhood—but the import of others is only revealed in the fullness of time. Trivia is the keeper of the turning points we can see only in retrospect: the lead or suggestion ignored or followed, the lover spurned or accepted, the opportunity taken or rejected. She helps us gather all of our strengths to negotiate these passages, and encourages our understanding. She is an active principle not simply because "not to decide is to decide," but because choosing creates opportunity. Choice, she tells us, can be nerve-wracking and terrifying (the light at the crossroads is almost always dim), but is ultimately empowering because it puts us in charge of our own destinies.

In that sense, Trivia is also the guardian of possibilities, because it is only at the crossroads of life that we can envision a tomorrow different from today. The crossroads is the place where dreams can intersect with reality, where the unconscious is forced into consciousness by choice. Reclaiming Trivia as a guardian—she who was "trivialized" by the patriarchy over time—can help us recognize the half-hidden or completely obscured opportunity at every fork in the journey of life. She and her torch represent another type of illumination.

Invoke Trivia by seeing choice as positive in nature—no matter how anxiety prone or unsure you are. We instinctively shy away from the "either/or" the crossroads represents, but Trivia lets us see past our fear of the unknown, our comfort on the trodden path, and can help free us to become risk takers in the best of all senses.

Robert Frost's poem "The Road Not Taken" perfectly sums up the challenges of the crossroads. Make a copy of it and tape it up somewhere prominent so you'll be able to see it every day. Trivia will be there, torch in hand, right by your side.

The Road Not Taken

Two roads diverged in a yellow wood,
And sorry I could not travel both
And be one traveler, long I stood
And looked down one as far as I could
To where it bent in the undergrowth;

Then took the other, as just as fair,
And having perhaps the better claim,
Because it was grassy and wanted wear;
Though as for that, the passing there
Had worn them really about the same,

And both that morning equally lay
In leaves no step had trodden black.
Oh, I kept the first for another day!
Yet knowing how way leads on to way

I doubted if I should ever come back.

I shall be telling this with a sigh
Somewhere ages and ages hence;
Two roads diverged in a wood, and I—
I took the one less traveled by,
And that has made all the difference.

Commitment
Hestia

While Hestia is primarily the deity of the home and household, she also represents the power of commitment—the promises we keep to ourselves and others. Her symbol is the enduring flame—the fire of warmth and safety—and her shrine is the hearth that feeds body and soul. Hestia's fire was kept ever burning by the Greeks; if it went out, it could only be rekindled by friction or the rays of the sun reflected through glass. Her flame signified continuity and community; the Greeks carried torches from the homeland to light the hearth fires on foreign shores. Hestia is a virgin goddess, signifying her independence and her unwavering commitment. In myth, she stays the course alone; unlike the other goddesses and gods, she never plays a role in wars or rivalries. In the ancient world, the first and last offerings were always made to her.

Hestia is the guardian to whom we turn when we question our life choices—those nagging "Is this what I signed up for?" moments—or when we can't remember why we first took the path we find ourselves on now. She is there when we feel over scheduled or simply undone by the routines of daily life—the balancing act of work and family or just the cycle of doing the dishes, paying the bills, taking out the trash. We can also call upon her when we need to commit to a different path that is new and untried but that will bring us closer to the literal and symbolic place we call "home."

Hestia began as the goddess of the family but came to be understood as presiding over the hearth of the earth and the universe. We can see her as exemplifying the web of relationship—the family we are born into as well as our chosen "family" of friends, lovers, partners, husbands, neighbors, and colleagues. All of these people—as well as the places we live—become the center of our spiritual "home," the place where we want to find ourselves, which is supported by commitment.

Help strengthen your ties and sense of belonging by getting rid of the clutter in your life—things, activities, even personal associations you've held on to but are no longer dedicated to. "Clutter" exists on a literal, psychological, and emotional level and often impedes true commitment. Work on the literal clutter first—it's the easiest to see and deal with—by paring down to the things you love and the things you need. Don't try to do it all at once—commitment takes time and effort. Next, look at how you spend your time and ask yourself whether you feel truly connected to each activity you participate in. If you do not, it's time to let go. Being "overcommitted" often reflects a lack of true dedication.

Honor Hestia by lighting candles and by concentrating on what you consider to be your spiritual home—the place where you'd like to live your life fully, surrounded by the people you love. Make a list of the people, principles, and activities you wish to commit to. Next to each entry on the list, write down the blessing or gift you have received in return for honoring your commitments. Every morning, read the list aloud—and add to it as Hestia stands by you and your sense of promise burgeons.

Compassion
Kuan Yin

This graceful goddess is a protector from whom mercy flows as bountifully as the waters of life contained in the vase she carries. For more than two thousand years, Kuan Yin has comforted the suffering, provided succor to infertile women, protected the souls of children, rescued the shipwrecked, and brought rain and water—metaphorically and literally—to parched earth and throats. She is invoked in times of danger and need. In Chinese, her name means "Hearer of Cries," while its Sanskrit meaning is "Born of the Lotus." Once envisioned as a male disciple of Buddha, in time her special compassion became understood as divinely feminine. Thus she is usually pictured as a beautiful woman, nude or clad in white, with a child in her arms, standing or sitting on a lotus; she often wears pearls and a rosary and holds a branch of the water-loving willow. The branch symbolizes flexibility, purification, and her connection to the spirit world.

Different sacred stories paint her as a benevolent and

often self-sacrificing guardian. In one, Kuan Yin began life as Miao-Shan ("wonderously kind"), the daughter of a controlling and worldly king who opposed her wish to enter a convent. She disobeyed him, and the king used every means at his disposal to dissuade her. At the king's command, the rigors of convent life were increased hundredfold. And even though Miao-Shan was given every degrading and unpleasant task, she stayed the course. Unable to wear her down, her father finally ordered her death, but the sword held by the executioner shattered into a thousand pieces. Instead, she was suffocated and went straight to the underworld, where her presence immediately doused the flames and caused flowers to bloom. The lord of the underworld, seeing his domain turned into a paradise, sent Miao-Shan back to the land of the living; cradled in the heart of a lotus, she was carried to the sacred mountain on the island of Potalaka. In time, her father became gravely ill, and in an act of forgiveness and filial piety, Miao-Shan sacrificed her eyes and the flesh of her arms so that he could be cured. The king was restored to health by her act, and, in gratitude, he commissioned a statue of his daughter, reminding the sculptor to portray her with "fully formed eyes and arms." Somehow, the sculptor misunderstood and rendered her with a thousand arms and eyes, as she is usually portrayed in China.

Because Kuan Yin forsakes anger or revenge toward her father and, instead, treats him with compassion, she is the guardian to whom we turn when we find our own hearts hardened by experience or when we are caught in the snare of self-involvement. The need to be strong and look out for ourselves sometimes has a cost: we can become deaf to the cries we need to hear. At these times, we look to Kuan Yin for inspiration. She can help soften the part of us that is too judgmental and exacting. She can help us relearn the true meaning of the word *compassion*—derived from the Latin *com* or "together" and *pati*, "to suffer." Neither empathy nor sympathy, it signifies oneness with another's pain.

Begin by letting go of what has hardened your heart so that you can let Kuan Yin into your life. You may want to cast these experiences out symbolically, writing them on slips of paper and burning them in a fireproof bowl. Or you may want to visualize Kuan Yin as flowing water; imagine the water flowing over your body, and try to visualize becoming one with it. Let the protective boundaries of the self dissolve. If you have a fountain, you can use it to help you meditate and visualize, or you can take a ritual bath to rid yourself of emotional calluses. Set aside time when you won't be disturbed. Light candles around the bath, make the water comfortably warm, and add bath salts or other aromatics.

Once you feel open to her influence, shift your focus to someone who needs the benefit of your compassionate strength. Write a prayer of healing for him or her, and make the power of Kuan Yin your own.

Divorce
The Wolf

This guardian isn't the "big bad wolf" immortalized in fairy tales as the representative of untrammeled instinct and ferocity, but the teacher and sage who draws on life experience to inform her actions, and who also exemplifies maternal instinct. Divorce is a special circumstance—an emotional and legal event, as well as a process—that requires special skills, sagacity, and a sense of balance. Roughly half of the women reading these pages will experience it in their lifetimes, many of them mothers. Their children will also experience and be shaped by divorce.

During separation and divorce, we can benefit from the wolf's ability to navigate and claim new territory as well as from her worldly wisdom. The timberland wolf, for example, doesn't enter her den during a blizzard—the den is reserved for birth and the protection of cubs—but instead she lies down in the snow, covering her nose and paws with her tail, and allows the snow to insulate her from the cold. She doesn't ignore the elements but uses them to serve her own purpose; so too, during divorce, we must learn to use the elements of the storm around us to our advantage and purpose. The wolf quickly familiarizes herself with her territory to maximize her safety and that of her cubs; in the same way, no matter how changed we find the circumstances of our lives, we have to lay claim to them.

Divorce entails a series of decisions, and we will have to avail ourselves of long-term vision, particularly if we have children—making sure that we aren't acting out of anger or hurt, or looking for redress. We need to be realistic and protective of ourselves. Wolf exhibits finely honed instincts as a member of the pack, a nurturer, and a hunter. She knows how to recognize and size up her prey, and will back down or rely on the combined strength of the pack if an adversary appears to be too strong or capable of inflicting injury. She is never impetuous. We will need Wolf's ability to assess our situation and to gauge when and whether we need help in handling things, large and small. The wolf's ability to know when to back down from a fight may come in handy, too, if the divorce becomes intensely adversarial.

The tremendous adjustment both during and after divorce—the assumption of all responsibilities where there was once a division of labor, as well as increased financial burdens—may leave many women feeling as though they are totally alone and afraid. Here, too, Wolf has lessons to teach us about the value of relying on our "pack." She reminds us to seek help for ourselves and our children if we need it and that there is no special benefit or virtue in going the course alone.

In her book, *Women Who Run with the Wolves*, Clarissa Pinkola Estés identifies the wolf as the "wilderness" within every woman, the ancient spirit of "The One Who Knows," whose "home is that place in time where the spirit of women and the spirit of wolf meet—the place where mind and instincts mingle, where a woman's deep life funds her mundane life." Do read her book if you feel you need help accessing the wolf within you. As Estés writes, this "wild nature" is ours to claim, for "among wolves, no matter how sick, no matter how cornered, no matter how alone, afraid, or weakened, the wolf will continue. She will lope even with a broken leg. She will go near others seeking the protection of the pack. She will strenuously outwait, outrun, outwit, and outlast whatever is bedeviling her. . . . The hallmark of the wild nature is that it goes on. It perseveres." We can learn from Wolf as Estés describes her by believing that it is in our nature to reach within for the wisdom to help us thrive, no matter what. The circumstances of divorce are a special wilderness—each divorce unique in its own way. That said, there are general lessons from which every woman can benefit.

Divorce as an event requires your full attention to detail, and while Wolf should guide your spirit, your energies need to be devoted to finding the best counsel and the most productive solutions to the problems at hand. Familiarize yourself with all the issues pertaining to divorce—whether to pursue mediation, for example, or the terms and conditions of alimony and child support—so that you make informed choices.

Never, ever, hesitate to ask for help.

Exploration
The Dolphin

Playful and gregarious, the dolphin has long been considered a sacral creature. The dolphin was associated with many of the Greek gods and goddesses—the sea god Poseidon, the messenger Hermes, Aphrodite, Eros, Demeter in her aspect as "Mistress of the Waters," and Apollo. Even though she was thought to be a fish, the womb and lactating breasts of this sea mammal added to her mystery and connected her to the realm of humanity and the great Earth Mother. It was said that when Apollo established the oracle in Delphi, dolphins carried his followers there from Crete. The dolphin's ability to plumb the depths of the waters and then to leap into the sky symbolized both profound wisdom and prophesy. Her great speed and her extraordinary agility—breaching, turning, spinning in the air with ease—made her the master navigator, the supreme voyager, and the sailor's companion. In Greek and Etruscan mythology, dolphins were the divine steeds of the waters, carrying the gods as well as the dead to the Blessed Isles. They rescued both heroes and sailors from drowning. Christian tradition has incorporated many of these older meanings; the dolphin symbolizes salvation, carrying souls to heaven, and serves as an emblem of Christ and the Resurrection.

Dolphin's abilities give us confidence to explore the waters of relationship and to open ourselves to exploration with our partners. She tells us to be playful and to enjoy ourselves, especially on the physical level. Her easy companionship helps pull us out of our shell and lets us see new possibilities for connection and pleasure. As a social animal who never travels alone, she encourages us to explore new relationships and to widen our circle of friends. She urges us to communicate—to laugh and play, to move freely in the world—without hesitation. She is the guardian of the positive outlook and reminds us that the glass is always half-full, never half-empty.

You can invite the spirit of Dolphin into your life in many ways and on many levels. Explore new ways of connecting to your partner sensuously and sexually. (Cathy Winks and Anne Semans's book *Sexy Mamas: Keeping Your Sex Life Alive While Raising Kids* is a good resource for mothers.) If you feel as though there isn't enough Dolphin energy in your life, get out into the world more often and meet people; join a health club, get involved in volunteer work, or start a reading group.

Wear a piece of dolphin-inspired jewelry to remind yourself that life is meant to be enjoyed and let the spirit of this glorious creature pervade your life. Dolphin reminds us that we have to lighten up now and again and explore new possibilities.

Love
Aphrodite

Although we tend to think of Aphrodite as the goddess of romantic and sexual love, the Greeks understood her as having many aspects, and their vision of Aphrodite's divine energy has much to teach us. Scholars agree that this goddess was most probably not original to the Greek pantheon; her worship might have originated in Cyprus or in Mesopotamia. According to sacred stories, she was born when her sky god father's genitals were cast into the ocean—her name means "of the sea foam"—at a time when Heaven and Earth were not yet separated. In *The Myth of the Goddess: Evolution of an Image*, Anne Baring and Jules Cashford brilliantly observe, "In this sense Aphrodite is 'born' when people joyfully remember, as a distinct and sacred reality, the bonds that exist between human beings and animals and, indeed, the whole of nature. The myth proposes that this happens through love."

And it is love as the remembrance of original oneness that resonates through the rites and places sacred to Aphrodite; sexual love is an important, but not the exclusive, aspect of this oneness. Her connection to the waters suggests her elemental nature, and in this aspect she is seen as a protector. With the dolphin as her attribute, she was invoked as "She Who Rises from the Sea," "The Giver of Prosperous Voyagers," and "The Goddess of Fair Weather." Her realm also extended to the netherworld, land of the dead; as "Aphrodite of the Tomb," she graced a site at Delphi where libations were offered to the dead. Similarly, she was also known as "The Goddess of the Depths," suggesting that the bonds of love—indeed, the need for the connection love represents—do not end with the tomb. Love is the sacred energy essential to rebirth; each year, Aphrodite's statue was ceremoniously bathed, and she was believed to emerge as a virgin once again.

She was also the goddess of fruitfulness, of sexual desire, and the act of procreation, which yields increase. In this aspect, she was hailed as the "Flower Goddess," "Aphrodite in the Garden," "She of the Marsh," or "Goddess of the Bank of Reeds." As the goddess of love in all of its aspects, she was also invoked as a protector of birth and family life: as Aphrodite Genetyllis ("Bringing about Birth"), as Aphrodite Tenetrix ("Joiner in Marriage"), as Aphrodite Nymphia ("Bridal Goddess"), and as Aphrodite Kourotrophos ("Rearer of Boys"). As the goddess of sexual desire, both sacred stories and rites attested to her primacy. Her girdle made anyone who wore it irresistible, and her temples were graced by sacred courtesans. She was also the goddess of joy and laughter, attended by the Hours—the goddesses of the seasons—and the Three Graces.

In time, Aphrodite was understood as having two major aspects: Aphrodite Urania ("She Whose Seat Is in Heaven") and Aphrodite Pandemos ("Of the People"). By the fourth century BCE, the Platonic writings presented these two aspects of love—the heavenly, or "sacred," type, which included the passion for ideas, and the earthly, or "profane," type, which included sexual passion—as separate but still connected. It's worth remarking that the highest ideal of Platonic love was love between men—a reflection of women's disenfranchisement from sacral life and Aphrodite's demotion from goddess to abstraction. The Christian tradition would sever the connection between sacred and profane love entirely and view them as opposed archetypes.

By reclaiming Aphrodite as the guardian of love, we can begin to restore a vision of wholeness that connects the many different kinds of love we feel for people, creatures, and things. She is a guardian of wholeness, permitting us to see our womanhood as integrated and our sexuality as connected to all the other kinds of love we feel, including maternal love. The idea of celebrating love as a sacred "reunion" is a valuable perception in a culture that has ambivalent feelings about women's sexuality. Aphrodite can be especially helpful during the child-rearing years, when the passions and needs of the individual and the couple are often sacrificed. Aphrodite reminds us that being a "good" mother needs to be integrated within the larger context of love within our lives. She reminds us that time spent in bed with a loving partner is part of that picture.

Aphrodite's lesson is simple: love and loving are part of wholeness. Honor love as a "sacred reality" in your daily life, and celebrate the emotional and physical connections that form the bonds of relationship. The rose is sacred to Aphrodite, and the flower itself—praiseworthy not only for its glorious scent and color—symbolizes the unity of love (the flower), which encompasses many elements (the petals). Meditate upon a single rose to bring Aphrodite into your life; look into the heart of the flower and rediscover the profound mystery and magic of love.

Marriage
Hera

Long before she was turned into the bickering, jealous, and avenging wife of the philandering Zeus in myth and story, the Greek Hera was venerated in sanctuaries and sacred rites. An ancient goddess whose temples are among the oldest and largest, she was the guardian of women, of the sacred union of marriage, of sexual and emotional intimacy, and of commitment. Her name means "lady," and it seems likely that she once was associated with the earth. She remained connected to the fertility of women both as the mother of Eileithyia, goddess of childbirth, and the patron of laboring women. While the Hera of myth can be seen as a negative patriarchal archetype—an embittered divine hausfrau who can neither live with Zeus nor without him—the goddess we glimpse in the art and ruins of her sanctuaries is something else entirely.

Rituals performed by her acolytes reflected her three aspects: Hera Parthenos, the child or unmarried maiden; Hera Teleia, "The Grown or Fulfilled One"; and Hera Chera, the widow. These three aspects reflected the life stages and passages of those dedicated to her and may have connected to the seasons as well as lunar phases: the spring of the maiden, or crescent moon; the summer of the wife, or full moon; the winter of the widow, or dark moon. But most importantly, these stages of womanhood defined by relationship—two periods of self-sufficiency bracketing one of union—were not understood as separate but as connected and cyclical. Each year at the new moon, women ritually celebrated Hera's return to her maiden state by bathing in the holy Imbrasos River on the island of her birth, Samos. The sacred marriage between Zeus and Hera was reenacted in ceremony every six years. The Heraion, the goddess's precinct, was active from Mycenaean through Roman times.

The ancient rites celebrating Hera teach an important truth about marriage: even though we are in an important, defining, and transforming relationship, we must retain our essential selves. The dyad of wife and husband can only thrive if each is whole unto him- or herself. The yearly return to maidenhood—the self untouched—can be understood as a ritual renewal of passion, a sloughing off of routine and negative experience, a rejuvenation of energy, or a return to the "you" who first met your husband-to-be. This goddess helps us understand the cycles that govern not only our own development but the marriage itself. Hera's wisdom lets us see marriage not as linear—a straight path with a few hills and valleys from our wedding days to today—but as cyclical. Like the moon's own cycle, your marriage may pass into periods of "darkness"—when all the energy of your connection to each other seems spent—and, following the lunar example, the two of you must use your own efforts to renew that energy again. While Hera can inspire, remember that the real work of renewal must be done by both members of the dyad.

In these postfeminist times, Hera can also remind us that dedicating ourselves to marriage and partnership—making a life with someone who is loved, honored, and respected just as we are loved, honored, and respected—is a worthy goal founded in strength, rather than a sign of weakness or insecurity.

Honor Hera by creating an altar symbolizing marriage and its cycles. If you are married, place pictures of your life together—from your wedding day to now, with all the times in between—on the altar, along with objects you associate with your marriage. Use two of everything, if you can, to symbolize the dyad. Hera's own symbols include the color red, the pomegranate, the willow, the lily, lilies of the valley, and the peacock. You can also add objects that symbolize growth and change—such as moonstones, acorns, seeds, eggs, or egg-shaped objects— to signify potential.

If you are in a relationship and considering getting married, use your journal to explore your feelings and thoughts about the commitment marriage represents. Write about how you think the dyadic partnership will change and enrich your life and his. Encourage your partner to explore his feelings as well, and spend time discussing what you each have discovered.

Motherhood
The Virgin Mary

Descendant of the ancient, pre-Christian mother goddesses, Mary reflects humanity's deep longing for unconditional love, unquestioning devotion, and inexhaustible caring. Understanding the "perfect motherhood" she has reflected for over two thousand years can help us negotiate the myths of maternity that still animate so many contemporary discussions about what mothering is and ought to be, and that many of us personal worry and anguish. Even though her doctrinal image has been rightly identified as a weapon in the patriarchal arsenal used to keep women in their "place," her story nonetheless captures an essential human truth about motherhood. Like all of us, she gives birth and embarks on a journey that is largely unknown and that, in the fullness of time, will yield both joy and pain. Since she herself, is in part, a cultural artifact—created out of the need to find an "ideal" answer to life's dilemmas—she can help us through the tangle of ideas that define the "Perfect Mother." She can help us distinguish the unhealthy pressures we feel from the real work of raising our daughters and sons.

The Virgin Mary of the poets and painters is, by turns, transcendent, yet of this earth; serene, yet wracked by pain; human, yet touched by miracle; protector of the meek and humble on Earth, yet "Queen of Heaven" in all her majesty. Ancient associations with the divine feminine—the mother goddesses—became her attributes; like them, she would have the moon beneath her feet, be seated on a throne of lions, embrace all flora and fauna, and be recognized as the source of all sustenance, spiritual and physical. The books of the New Testament tell her sacred story, but despite the richness of Mary's legacy and the fullness of her portrait in art and literature, she is mentioned only nineteen times. In fact, the Bible yields few details about her. We do not know who her parents were, what she looked like, how old she was, how she married Joseph, or even when she died. We do know of the travail that preceded and followed her son's birth, but know nothing of how she raised him. She is present at only one of the miracles, that of the marriage at cana. Only one gospel locates her at the foot of the cross. The risen Christ does not appear to her.

And yet she emerged as the Perfect Mother through

myth and legend, which added the details the canonical story left out. These details—two thousand years of them— influence our beliefs about what motherhood entails, whether we believe in Mary or reject her outright. Her mythic image—all caring, unconditionally loving, consoling, protecting, embracing, and sacrificing—provides the background to everything we think we know or believe about motherhood.

Many of us find that becoming a mother raises questions we never expected to have to answer. We may continue to work—by choice or necessity—and find ourselves wondering whether we are failing our children as a result. Or we may decide to stay at home and feel, somehow, that we are failing ourselves by giving up the opportunities the outside world offers us.

Our choices may lead us to question the models of behavior we present to our children. Few of us, no matter what we choose, will find our lives or our ways of mothering "perfect," and perhaps the first step Mary can help us take is to recognize that "perfection" exists only in the imagination.

Understanding the role Mary has played in the cultural imagination can help stimulate a more fruitful dialogue among us about the choices we make—whether to be a working or stay-at-home mother,—and the ways our choices affect our children.

The care with which Mary's portrait as a mother was burnished over the course of two millennia suggests that the Perfect Mother, in her earthly incarnation, has always been elusive. Whether she inspires or infuriates, Mary is there to remind us that the journey we undertake as mothers is an ancient and universal one, and that we can best undertake it in each other's company.

Negotiation
Ganesh

His devotees begin every undertaking by invoking the "Lord of the Hosts," the meaning of his name in Sanskrit. Ganesh is the Hindu god of wisdom and art, depicted with an elephant's head and a human body. He is the remover of obstacles, always pictured as plump and rounded, signifying prosperity, and—incongruously but meaningfully—seated on a mouse or rat. His elephant nature gives him strength and physical power; the elephant, after all, can uproot any trees in its path, trample brush and grasses, ford streams and rivers, and use its mighty weight to subdue the elements. The mouse, on the other hand, is possessed of agility and able to squeeze itself into the smallest of spaces, and thus signifies that Ganesh can enter everywhere. Ganesh's choice of the lowly mouse as his steed demonstrates his humility and tells us that, despite his girth, Ganesh isn't ponderous or heavy handed, but is light in spirit. Similarly, his large ears symbolize that he listens intently to all; his broken tusk connotes sacrifice; the sweetmeat he holds in his trunk reflects the sweetness of life. His four arms hold his other attributes, among them a shell, a discus, a goad, and a water lily.

There are several versions of the story of how Ganesh got his elephant head. In one, Ganesh was created by his mother, Parvati, who had him stand guard at the door while she bathed; Shiva, her husband, became furious when he saw Ganesh there and cut off his head. To appease Parvati, Shiva promised to replace her son's head with that of the first sleeping creature he saw—which was an elephant.

Ganesh is the perfect guardian of negotiation because he emphasizes that, to reach agreement, we must remove any obstacles and let go of the need to win each point. The key to a successful negotiation is remembering that both parties must leave satisfied without feeling vanquished. Women often have trouble negotiating on their own behalf; they may waiver between trying to please the other party, on the one hand, and feeling as though they need to win, on the other.

Remember that our word *negotiate* means both to reach a settlement, or compromise, and to succeed in crossing, or getting past, an obstacle or a hazard—as in "negotiating" turbulent waters. Invoke Ganesh and visualize the obstacles you need to get past to arrive at agreement. Try to see the obstacles as three-dimensional—actual, physical things in your way—so that you can better understand them. All negotiations will benefit from your efforts to understand both your own underlying motivations and attitudes as well as those of the other party. Visualize the situation from the other person's point of view and see how you can anticipate his or her objections to or reservations about the solution you've proposed. By anticipating the other person's reactions or questions, you may well be able to remove all or most of the obstacles at hand. Similarly, visualize what you perceive to be obstacles— and make sure that they are not obstacles you've created for yourself. Ganesh helps us realize that different negotiations require different skills: do you need the obvious and sometimes overwhelming strength of the elephant or do you want to call on the agility of the mouse? Keep in mind that the quiet mouse can sometimes gain entry to places where the elephant's trumpeting strength is of no use. Remember that Ganesh is humble, not a show-off; is your own pride or your need to prove a point getting in your way?

Our culture tends to value "winning" above all, but the need to "win" usually doesn't serve us in negotiation— whether we are negotiating to buy or sell something, hammering out a divorce or employment agreement, or trying to settle disputes or differences equitably with a friend, partner, or spouse. Invoke Ganesh's lightness of being to get rid of the excess baggage you bring to the table, and invoke his powers of hearing to make sure that you truly listen to both yourself and the other person.

Most important, try to be flexible during the course of negotiation. Listen carefully and take your time as you decide how to respond. Ganesh will help show the way.

Nurturance
The Bear

We have proof that humanity's reverence for the bear goes back some fifty thousand years, but it doubtless began even earlier. The bear epitomized the superb navigator, the model warrior, the strong opponent, the cunning forager, and the skillful hunter. This earth-bound creature even had a heavenly presence in the constellations Ursa Major and Minor; the polestar, which guided travelers and navigators the world over, belonged to her. But it is as a dedicated and fierce mother that Bear is the guardian of nurturance: she who sleeps when the earth rests in winter and emerges from her cave with her cubs as the earth yields up its green shoots. Closely connected to the earth, birth, and regeneration, the bear is also a nurturer of the self; she hunts, forages, and feeds herself, building up layers of fat, in preparation for her hibernation and the birth of her offspring. She embodies the principle of self-sustenance, which, in turn, permits her to bear and nurture her young. As Paul Shepard and Barry Sanders point out in their book *The Sacred Paw:*

The Bear in Nature, Myth, and Literature, the many meanings that our word *bear* derives from its Indo-European roots are hardly accidental. Among these are "to bring forth or give birth," "to support or maintain," "to have fortitude," "to orient," and "to keep in mind."

We turn to Bear when we need to nurture ourselves and require a respite, just for a moment, from the task of taking care of others. Bear supports us in our goal of being the best mother, daughter, sister, friend, and teacher of life skills we can be—and fortifies us when we get home from work too tired to cook or when we just don't have the patience to help with homework. She reminds us that to be nurturing, we must first nurture ourselves. She props us up when all we need to do simply becomes too much.

Because her cubs are born hairless, blind, and disproportionately tiny—looking nothing like the bears they will become—the bear's ability to nurture inspired awe; she was thought to lick and mold her formless offspring into their ursine shape. The cub's utter dependency on its mother made the bear the Madonna of the beasts, as did the time cubs take to mature; even though they are noisy and demanding, older cubs need a fierce protector against predators, including male bears. Great healing powers as well as extensive herbal knowledge—she knows where to find the tastiest and newest shoots and leaves—were imputed to the bear by diverse cultures, and are still reflected in many common names of plants. Among them are bear bane (*Aconitum*), bear's breech (*Acanthus*), bear's paw (*Cotyledon tomentosa*), bear's foot (*Helleborus foetidus*), and bear's garlic (*Allium ursinum*). Many Native Americans understood tobacco, the sacred plant of the Americas, to be closely connected to the bear as healer. Elsewhere, ursine shapes and characteristics animate ancient visions of the divine mother and the feminine force; an image of a bear mother nursing her cub survives from 5,000 BCE, while young Athenian girls donned bearskins every fifth year to honor the goddess Artemis at Brauron in her aspect as the protector of women and animals in childbirth. The rites symbolically imitated childbirth, the life passage that every woman experiences alone, the first test of motherhood.

Follow the Bear Mother's example by nurturing yourself in body and spirit. Do something for yourself that gives you pleasure or comfort. It can be anything—a massage, a day alone in the country, or a lunch with friends. Schedule these moments as carefully as you schedule everything else that has to do with others.

Honor Bear in all her fullness by taking pride in all

you do to nurture others, but, at the same time, respect your own limits. Give up the ideal of the Perfect Mother who is all things to everyone. If you can't take on another task or responsibility, don't, and divert the energy you might spend feeling guilty into a positive focus. Pay attention to what you are already doing—and do your very best. If your weekday schedule doesn't permit you to cook the kind of meals you'd be serving in an ideal world, don't waste your time and energy worrying about it. Focus on simple, healthy meals instead—and make a more elaborate meal as part of a weekend family night.

As mothers, most of us find, at one point or another, that we would need another twelve hours in the day or a duplicate self to do all we would like to do. It's at those moments that Bear can be the most help.

Partnership
The Dyad

The dyad is the spirit as well as the guardian of partnership; reflecting the power of two, the dyad is almost always dynamic. A partnership may encompass the dualism implicit in the universe and be formed of two complementary opposites that, together, make the whole. A partnership may be composed of individuals so alike that their relation is one of reflection. Or the dyad may be extreme in its yoking of opposites—fractious and unstable—symbolizing the attraction of opposites. In this kind of partnership, the dyad is rarely made up of equals, and the connection is sometimes violent and always short lived. (The dyadic model here can be fire and water, for example; see the entry on "Passion" for more.)

Partnership includes many different kinds of relationships; dyads may be friends, lovers, spouses, or siblings. Partnerships formed for purposes other than mutual emotional sustenance or attraction—for business or convenience, for example—may still fall into the basic dyadic patterns. The world over, the dyad serves as a model of the universe itself. Its main hallmark is its fluidity; because the dyad contains two, it is always changing.

We can call upon the spirit of the dyad to help us improve our partnerships, to come to a better understanding of the role partnership plays in our lives, or, amidst a life passage, to discover new ways of making the partnerships more vital. The dyad has many names—and it is up to each of us to choose the partnership model that we find to be most productive.

The Chinese symbol of the dyadic whole is the yin/yang, symbolized by a circle divided by an S curve, one half white and the other black. Most importantly, within each half is a small circle of the opposite color— black within white, white within black. This small circle signifies interdependence and suggests that each half contains the seed of the other. Yin is black and stands for the feminine, the earth, intuitive thought, passivity, and softness. Yang is white and stands for the masculine, the sky, discursive reason, vitality, and hardness. But since each contains the seed of the other, the dyad is understood not as the yoking of opposites but as a fluid continuum. The partnership it describes is one in which roles can be flexible and interchangeable. The yin/yang partnership is the most durable but requires each member of the dyad to become a conscious complement of the other—letting go of traditional visions of what constitutes "masculine" or "feminine" behaviors. This model permits the dyad to weather periods of stress—the years of parenting or periods when one partner outearns the other—and requires mutual effort to let go of cultural norms and definitions.

Sacred stories from many cultures portray complementary dyadic partnerships as a way of providing answers to perceived dualisms such as life and death, fruition and dearth, wholeness and fragmentation. The pair may be mother and daughter, as in the story of Demeter and Persephone, or wife and husband, as in the story of Isis and Osiris. The reunion of the dyad symbolizes the oneness that integrates dualism.

In ancient Greece and Rome, the "twinned dyad"—the partnership of two so alike that they symbolize unity of thought and action—was "the Dioscuri," or the twins Castor and Pollux. When Castor was killed in battle, Pollux decided to join his brother in death, and Zeus placed the two in the heavens as the constellation Gemini. The Dioscuri were guardians of the land and sea—they protected travelers and sailors—as well as the gods of hospitality, oaths, and bonds. They thus represent the social stability of sameness. Twinned dyads can be friends, siblings, and sometimes spouses.

The work of strengthening a partnership can never be accomplished by one individual. But you can lay the groundwork for fruitful discussion by examining your own attitudes first. Try writing down what you consider to be the strengths and weaknesses of your connection—with the intention of sharing your words with your partner. In the best of all possible worlds, you will ask your partner to do the same. By considering how the yin/yang symbolizes a fluid partnership, determine the ways in which you are alike and different. This exercise can help you to see your differences as potential strengths.

Building an altar together can also help affirm your sense of commitment to the partnership while you continue to explore the ways in which the dyad can be made stronger. Using the theme of the yin/yang, choose objects to put on the altar. Choose objects that have personal resonance and try to explain to your partner why you have chosen them. Again, focus on the "seed" of the one that is in the other, and allow yourselves to become more aware of the unrealized potential in each other. Lighting candles together is also healing and renewing.

Passion
Pele

The primal Hawaiian goddess of the volcano, she is the spirit of fire—the burning, molten energy of earth—that eternally seeks to escape containment. Her essence explodes and bubbles out of the vents and fissures of the crater itself, sending up plumes of fire, smoke, and ash. Unappeasable in her desire, she mingles with her sometime lover Ocean, hissing and spitting, making the waters boil, destroying all in her path. Yet new land rises up out of the lava that flows from her center—she is simultaneously "The Shaper of the Sacred Land" and "She Who Devours the Land"—and she leaves behind traces of herself. Strands of glass formed of the molten mass are called "Pele's hair," while the small pieces of obsidian are known as "Pele's tears."

She is passion made manifest in all of its meanings: burning, primal, untamable, emboldening. She is the fire that feeds our emotions, causing us to shimmer with physical pleasure and glow with love. She is the fire in the belly that fuels all creative endeavors. Her ability to create something out of nothing—the land that rises out of the waters' depths—reminds us that we can only create when her special power is part of our lives.

But Pele's sacred stories are equally filled with anger, suspicion, and conflict, all of which coexist with intense sexual desire. It is no accident that her lovers are those with whom union is achieved only at great cost and with destructive consequences.

As exemplified by this goddess, passion's creative essence cannot be fully separated from its destructive capacities. The bright flame of our passion leaves us vulnerable to hurt and pain; the intensity of feeling may render us incapable of shifting our attention elsewhere, even when it is needed. Passion is the fulcrum for the greatest of love stories as well as the source of all tragedy, real or imagined; no other emotion has the ability to lift us so high or to tumble us so low.

A volatile spirit, Pele can never be invoked halfheartedly. You may want to relinquish her hold on your life if the passion you feel has nothing left but destructive energy. Rituals can help you to cede your anger, bitterness, and hostility back to Pele. Write down the words and thoughts you carry with you and burn the paper in a fireproof bowl. Let the curling and charred pieces signify your release from Pele's power. Tear or break objects you associate with your passion to signify your breaking away from its hold, and remove these objects from the altar. Cover red objects, symbolizing fire and passion, with cloths of blue or white, emblems of reason and clarity. Recognizing the destructive aspect of your own emotions is the first step in walking away from the power Pele has over your life.

Sexual passion can sometimes be part of Pele's transformative but destructive domain. If sexual passion has become part of a cycle of self-destruction, you will need to decide if you want your life ruled by the unpredictable power of fire.

Patience
The Tortoise

It's little wonder that so many cultures assumed the universe rested on her back or that her legs were the pillars supporting the cosmos. In China, the curve of the tortoise's shell was an emblem of heaven, while her underside signified earth; her body symbolized humankind held between heaven and earth. Slow and deliberate, she is possessed of great strength and stability; carrying her armor and shelter on her back, she is an emblem of order that cannot be challenged or changed by attack, and of a world vision that isn't dependent on bravado or ego. Her remarkable longevity associates her with the wisdom of the elders, as well as the long view of life and time. In Aesop's fable, the speedy braggart hare dares the tortoise to race him. In the end, the hare is beaten by his own arrogance—he naps while the tortoise plods toward the finish line—and the tortoise wins by dint of her perseverance and her understanding of the hare's shortcomings.

Tortoise represents a vision of life grounded in eternal rhythms, which permits us to be patient. She is the antidote to a culture that idolizes the "quick study" and the star of the "fast track," and that promotes every product as "instant," "time saving," or "easy." She reminds us that profound wisdom is rarely possessed quickly or easily but usually emerges slowly over time. Her motto might well be *festina lente*—"Make haste slowly"—Augustus Caesar's invocation against impetuousness or rushing. In the Renaissance, this motto was often illustrated with a picture of a turtle with a sail, moving slowly through the waters, completely on course.

Make room in your life for Tortoise when you've become the woman leaning on the horn, when interrupting others mid-sentence has become a way of life, or when you find yourself muttering every time something takes a minute more than you expected. You need to take off your running shoes—literally and metaphorically—and let life develop at its own pace.

Honor patience and the rhythm of slow unfolding by walking a labyrinth—many churches have one—or, if you have a garden or patio, create one out of pebbles and rocks. Take a long, meandering walk on a sunny day with no particular agenda or timetable; let the rhythms of your footfalls become the beat of a new way of moving through time and space.

Let other, larger rhythms—not just the sixty-second minute or the sixty-minute hour—begin to emerge as a new pattern in your life. Sometimes patience simply needs a foundation; think of it as a lesson you once learned but have since forgotten. Give yourself a new awareness of time. Plant some seeds or pits indoors or out, and use your journal to record their growth each day. Take a walk through your neighborhood, no matter what the season, and record the changes you see in nature each day—from the sky and clouds to the trees, grass, and flowers. Or walk under the night sky, and use your journal to describe the details that emerge from the darkness. Make room for the things you'd like to accomplish but that take patience—the half-finished afghan, the photo album—and discover the pleasure of work done well at a slower pace.

"Fast" and "easy" have become a contemporary mantra, probably because so many of us are always rushing from one thing to another. Time has become a precious commodity, and sometimes it feels as though patience is just an indulgence. But remember that patience yields the most beautiful of gardens, the intricacy of the tapestry, and the soft gleam of often-polished wood.

Reconciliation
The Rainbow

Whether we picture it as the lovely winged Greek goddess Iris, clad in shimmering garments with a caduceus in her hand, or see it simply as a manifestation of beauty and spirit, the rainbow is the guardian of reconciliation. Iris was the messenger and intermediary between the gods and mortals, and, the world over, the rainbow is seen as a bridge or passageway linking the earth and sky, symbolizing universal harmony as well as good fortune. In the Old Testament, the rainbow is the sign of God's renewed covenant with humanity after the Great Flood. In China, the colors of the rainbow symbolized the reconciliation of the feminine and masculine, cold and hot, dark and light, inward and outward, cyclical and linear, in a single, shimmering form. Our contemporary use of the rainbow as an image of diversity within unity stems from all of these traditions.

The rainbow thus becomes our model when we need to weave the threads of life or relationship back together after disruption or conflict. Its separate colors remind us that, within the unified whole, there are still meaningful differences and that, to be fully reconciled, we must honor and respect them. The seven colors of the rainbow—red, orange, yellow, green, blue, indigo, violet—each have symbolic associations, and thus the rainbow represents a balance of emotional states and attitudes. (Red is the color of passion and energy, for example, while blue is that of intellect and clarity; in the rainbow, they are reconciled and balanced by violet, which symbolizes moderation and spirituality.) It is important to remember that there are many other colors within the continuum that the human eye can't discern.

Use the rainbow as a starting point for a journal entry about the conflict you wish to end, describing the threads or events that brought the situation to a head. Assign each a color and see if, through writing about what has happened, you can create a rainbow of reconciliation. Or you can create an altar dedicated to reconciliation to inspire you to move forward. Use different-colored stones to represent the differences you have had, and build them into a rainbow-like arc. Or use objects symbolizing opposition—black and white, sweet and salty, soft and hard—and place them in twos, side by side. Add yellow objects to signify illumination or light a candle as you affirm your willingness to set aside your differences and seek reconciliation:

> I choose to let go of the past and the differences
> that drove us apart. I willingly and hopefully choose
> a new pathway of harmony.

You can also write your past grievances down on slips of paper and burn them in a fireproof bowl, affirming your commitment to let go of the past. Make two bracelets of multicolored thread or ribbons and plait them together to symbolize the rainbow; put one on your wrist and give the other to the person with whom you are reconciled.

Sincerity
Maat

The dictionary tells us what *sincerity* means: being truthful, honest, genuine. But the dictionary doesn't tell us how to live a sincere life. Can we live sincerely on every level, we wonder? It seems to require so much of us: true self-knowledge, unshakable conviction, a trustworthy inner compass. Despite these doubts, we also know that sincerity is the foundation of true happiness and peace. Without sincerity, we can't live comfortably in our skins nor can we trust ourselves to the care of others. Sincerity is the essential foundation of self and relationship; it is at the center of any dyad based on friendship or love. Precious and potent, sincerity can only grow in the garden of the soul when it is tended with a regimen of good intentions and discipline. We sometimes forget to remember sincerity as a blessing until we discover its absence.

We turn to the ancient Egyptian goddess Maat to help us cultivate this most important of qualities. Her name means "straight" or "level" (like the tool used by a carpenter); she was both a deity and a principle of the universe. The word *Maat* referred both to the physical order of the universe—she dictated the rising and setting of the sun, as well as its movement from east to west—and to the moral order. All rituals began by honoring her, the "true course." Representations of Maat were placed on the tongues of the dead so that their words would resonate with truth; as the principle of moral order, she weighed each heart against the weight of her feather in her scales of justice. Only those whose souls were as light as the feather were granted eternal life. Judges in the courts were considered her priests and wore her ostrich plume on their robes. When Egyptians prayed to her, they also swore an oath of confession, testifying to their truthfulness in spirit and act. Those devoted to her forswore violence to people and animals, lying and cheating, taking unfair advantage of workers, hasty judgments, greed and covetousness, and stealing.

Use a feather to enlarge your understanding of Maat. The feather represents true balance, one side mirroring the other; like the bird, it symbolizes the connection between the worlds of action and thought, the material and the spiritual, earth and sky. The feather is also an emblem of the lightness of being that comes with truthfulness.

Reflect on the harvest of the genuine in your life. Bring to mind the earnest thoughts, truthful words, and committed feelings you and those close to you have expressed. Take stock of the potent magic of sincerity: its ability to make us feel safe and secure; its power to create the close bonds of friendship and love; its capacity to make our lives whole and harmonious. Balance these reflections against the cost and pain of dissembling.

Write a pledge to yourself to work harder at becoming whole with truthfulness, and begin each day by reading it aloud. Keep a journal recording your own efforts to become more wholly sincere, as well as the gifts and blessings that have flowed back to you from your genuine words, gestures, and actions.

Support
Penelope

Not a goddess but a woman, Penelope is a literary archetype, once part of Greek mythology and then finely drawn in the Greek epic poem attributed to Homer, *The Odyssey*. Although she is often derided as the long-suffering and "faithful" wife, who remains adamantly chaste while her husband, Odysseus, succumbs to various temptations on his way home, both her plight and, finally, her triumph in the story are intimately connected to the nature of commitment and support.

In the story, Odysseus leaves home to fight the Trojan War, which lasts ten years; left behind are Penelope and their infant son. The nine years after the war has ended— when Odysseus doesn't return and she has no word of him—present Penelope with her supreme challenge. In addition to the loneliness and sorrow she has faced from the day her husband left, she has to contend not simply with maintaining her home and child in her husband's absence but with fending off the attentions of a hundred suitors who wish to ascend to Odysseus's throne. She keeps the suitors at bay with various ruses, proving that she is as wily and resourceful as her heroic husband; her most singular ploy is to assert that she cannot marry until she has finished weaving a shroud for her ancient father-in-law, Laertes. Weaving—traditional women's work that symbolizes the fabric of connection and family life— becomes emblematic of another type of sacrifice, as each night Penelope unravels what she has woven that day. As Elizabeth Wayland Barber has pointed out, to make the ruse believable—and to have it work for close to four years—Penelope must have been weaving a "storytelling cloth," a pattern that incorporated myth and personal history. Symbolically, as she unravels the day's work each night, she keeps her own story with Odysseus open-ended. By sacrificing her work—all that signifies her own self-expression and creativity—she sets her own needs aside for those of Odysseus and their family.

Penelope exemplifies the cost of commitment—each night, she cries herself to sleep—as well as the rigors of supporting the bonds of home, family, and marriage when life gets in the way. Penelope's misery is real and palpable throughout the poem—she laughs only once—but it coexists with her commitment to and love for her husband. It is, on one level, an accurate vision of how taking on the supportive role can sometimes be the most difficult of journeys. Penelope's fidelity leaves her isolated in her present, inconsolable at the loss of her past, and without the hope of a future; rather than understanding this vision of faithfulness as simple Greek misogyny, we can recognize it as a portrait of the self suspended and postponed by the circumstances of life. Penelope's own needs, goals, and dreams are put on hold in the service of her commitment to her life with her husband. It's worth saying that she is made stronger, not diminished, by her choice.

At the very moment that Penelope can no longer put off choosing a new husband—at the start of the twentieth year since Odysseus left—he returns home. He is disguised as a beggar, and Penelope's recognition of him is slow in coming. But then an easy homecoming would whitewash the extent of the sacrifices Penelope made to sustain their mutual life and to allow Odysseus to return to it. In the poem, Penelope recognizes her husband fully and finally through an intimate secret—the nature of their marriage bed—that only Odysseus, as its architect and builder, could share with her. The bed is unmovable—carved out of a living tree—and firmly connected to the earth, a symbol of their love and partnership.

Penelope helps us acknowledge how hard the burden

of support really is, without lessening our commitment to provide it. Each of us reading these pages will pass through a stage in our lives when we are needed in a different way by someone we love and care about—and we will put our own needs on hold. At these moments, we will need to be supported even as we give support; Penelope teaches us that giving up the self—unraveling the tapestry of life we have patiently woven—is never easy.

Become the teller of your own story by coming to terms with your present while leaving your future an open possibility. Instead of focusing on the burdens the present has placed on you, pay attention to the strengths and abilities you've acquired by rising to the occasion. Take pride in your choice to put another first, and recognize that "this too shall pass."

Body and Spirit

Aging
The Crane

S he is all grace and beauty; it is no wonder that the crane is the revered emblem of longevity and health in the Far East and elsewhere. Ancient myths held that she could live hundreds, if not thousands, of years; in fact, her life span in the wild is usually an amazing thirty years. Her extraordinary flexibility and stamina—she can swim, fly, and run with agility and speed—symbolize the accretion of talent and experience over a lifetime, the wisdom that comes from having lived. The crane is native to all the continents save South America and Antarctica, and her migratory patterns are both astonishingly consistent (she migrates at the same time every year, a passage tripped by hormones) and inspiring; she can fly as fast as fifty-two miles an hour and can traverse mountain ranges by soaring to a height of twenty thousand feet. Thus, she is an emblem of the ever-changing seasons in all women's lives and our ability to go the long distance.

Despite their delicate beauty, cranes are hardly shy or retiring; they can be tough, territorial, and fearless when it comes to protecting what is theirs. The crane also signifies communication—the duet of notes between the female and male known as a "unison call" is one among many crane calls—as well as contemplation, based on her apparent serenity as she stands at rest or sleeps. Because cranes usually mate for life, she is also an emblem of fidelity and perseverance. Above all, the crane is a survivor, an omnivore who can easily adapt to new circumstances.

Crane is the much-needed guardian of aging, particularly in a culture that is overly focused on youth and beauty, and that deems that while men gain power and character as they age, women simply get "old." She reminds us that a life passage can also be seen as a moment to take wing, to allow ourselves to be inspired, not discouraged, by the changes in our bodies. She tells us that our life experience isn't baggage that we carry as extra weight, but the ballast we need to make the journey safely and happily. She tells us that we are strong enough to make the flight alone, but shows us that taking advantage of the updrafts will make the voyage more pleasant.

The crane's yearly migration echoes the cyclical nature of our bodies, which is why the ancient Egyptians and Greeks understood her to be a symbol of rebirth. Crane helps us see that every passage in our lives, including aging, is an opportunity to be reborn anew. Because our society lacks the rites and rituals that celebrate women's life passages—turning thirty, forty, or fifty; or leaving the years of childbearing behind to move into the years of perimenopause and menopause—many of us neglect to honor the process of aging as an act of becoming.

Bring Crane's special example into your life by celebrating your passages with loved ones or close friends. Don't feel as though you have to wait for a birthday or a specific milestone; these are ongoing processes, after all, and you should celebrate simply to acknowledge that your journey continues through time.

Hang an image of the crane in your bedroom to keep you company on this part of the journey, and, following her example, let the updrafts of life lift you high above the land to a new view.

Energy
The Tiger

S trong and powerful, the tiger is sometimes endowed with negative symbolism as a merciless beast of prey and a destructive force, but the tiger also represents the positive force of primal energy. In China, tigers symbolized the cosmic order; they stood guard against the forces of chaos at the center of the universe and at all four cardinal points. (The supreme yellow tiger, earth, occupied the center. The red tiger ruled the south, the summer, and was symbolized by the element of fire. The east, the spring, and all vegetation were the domain of the blue tiger. Finally, the white tiger was the guardian of the west, and autumn, whose element was metal.) In the bagua of feng shui, the white tiger is the guardian of the west, the area of harvest and creativity. Those born in the year of the tiger (1914, 1926, 1938, 1950, 1962, 1974, 1986, 1998) are considered to be strong and active leaders but may also be rash or impulsive. In Hinduism, the creative female power of Shakti is associated with the tiger on which she rides. In Buddhism, the tiger is an emblem of the power and energy of faith.

We can call upon the tiger's dynamism when we feel listless, when we are unable to get ourselves up and going, or when we're leaving too many things unfinished. Tiger helps us become conscious of our surroundings and reminds us to make sure that the energy where we live and work is free and flowing. Bright light and colors have a positive effect on our energy levels; vibrant colors such as red, yellow, or orange have been shown to stimulate and arouse the senses. Conversely, darkness and dark colors lower the spirits. Scent can also invigorate; try burning lemongrass, eucalyptus, or peppermint candles to perk yourself up. Objects that move in a breeze—wind chimes or even the fronds of a plant—can also increase the energy in a room. Pick up a book on feng shui or sacred space, if you don't already have one. (Try William Spear's *Feng Shui Made Easy*, Sarah Rossbach's *Feng Shui: The Chinese Art of Placement*, or Denise Linn's *Sacred Space: Cleaning and Enhancing the Energy of Your Home* for more suggestions.)

Exercise is another way of bringing energy into your life; if you don't have time to make it to the gym, make sure you are taking a brisk walk for at least fifteen minutes a day.

Sometimes, lack of energy may indicate that you are simply trying to do too much or that you've been thinking too hard about everything on that eternal to-do list. Tiger is primal and acts out of instinct—no rumination or second-guessing for her—and you should follow her example by switching your focus from thinking to doing. Prioritize your areas of concern—this isn't the time to think globally—and work on one at a time. Seize the opportunity to get proactive and spring into action.

For the moment, set aside your journal writing and any other activities that have you thinking, not doing. Visualize the tiger—magnificent in her power, her stripes rendering her invisible in the dappled sun of the jungle—and take on her awesome spirit.

Fruitfulness
Nut

S he is the great sky goddess of the Egyptians, the cre-
atrix sometimes pictured as a celestial cow but usually
envisioned as a slim nude woman whose body stretches and
arches over the body of the earth, her fingers and toes
touching the cardinal directions. We see her at the moment
when she has just separated from her partner, the earth, his
penis still erect, after the act of the first creation. And so the
Egyptians believed that it was from her lovemaking that all
further creation ensued—the gods and goddesses, men
and women, flora and fauna. Each day, the great sky
mother—her legs bespangled with the stars of night—
gave birth to Re, her sun-god son, and each night, he
returned to her womb.

Nut is ever-flowing fruitfulness; she gives birth to the
heat of the sun, and the rain flows from her breasts, nour-
ishing all growth. Her attribute was a jar of waters—she
was sometimes pictured upright, the jar upon her head—
symbolic of life, creation, and all fruition. Nut was both
birth and rebirth; in the form of the sycamore, her sacred

tree, she fed the souls of the dead. Caskets bore her image both on the base, facing upward, and on the inner lid, facing downward, so that the dead were literally and metaphorically held in her embrace. As Erich Neumann notes in *The Great Mother*, she is water above and water below, and "life is her child, a fish eternally swimming inside her."

Nut, the divine sky mother, reminds us that a woman's "fruitfulness" encompasses not just her ability to bear children but her ability to give birth throughout her lifetime to the fruits of imagination, thought, creativity, and transformation. Nut permits us to see fruitfulness encompassing all that we do; as the goddess of the sky, she tells us to reach for the stars. She gives us another context in which to understand what "being a woman" means.

Nut can be our guardian when we are having trouble conceiving a child or when we feel diminished because motherhood isn't a part of our lives. She stands by us when, as mothers, we find ourselves not as happy or satisfied as we thought we would be, or when our relationship to our child or children becomes difficult or painful. She can be a guide when we go through menopause as well. Nut lets us look at all of our accomplishments—the relationships we've forged, the work of our hearts and minds, the beauty we've created in our homes, the ways we have given back to the community—as evidence of our "fruitfulness."

Welcome Nut into your life with the power of affirmation. Complete the statement "I have conceived and brought to life . . ." in your own words. Visualize all of nature's fruits—pinecones, oranges, apples, rose hips, grapes, acorns, coconuts, the "wings" of maples and elms, and the "parachutes" of dandelions—and let yourself admire your own fruits in all their variety.

Walk under the sky—night or day, it belongs to Nut—and reclaim a sense of possibility and continuing productivity.

Future
Jana

The Roman Jana and her consort, Janus, were the guardians of new beginnings who stood watch over entrances, doors, and gates—both literal and metaphorical—and who gave the first month of our calendar year its name. Originally they may have been the god and goddess of light and the new day—counterbalancing Diana, goddess of the moon and night—but were eventually understood in a broader sense. They were always depicted as having two faces—one that looked back and the other forward—which may symbolize the understanding that past and future, beginnings and endings, are always connected. Alternatively, their two faces may suggest that prophesy, or foretelling the future, is based in knowledge of the past.

They epitomized the spirit of "opening," and their epiphany was the swinging gate, which opens both ways. The temple at the Roman Forum dedicated to Jana/Janus had its doors open in wartime and closed during times of peace; it's been suggested that the doors were open in wartime so that citizens defending the state would have free access to the city whether they returned victorious or vanquished. Similarly, the doors of private homes were left open when the occupants were away and were closed when they were home. Jana and Janus were worshipped not just at the beginning of the first month of the new year—with an offering of new meal, wine, frankincense, and salt—but in the first hour of each new day, before any other deity. No new enterprise, voyage, or effort began without first honoring them.

With Jana's guidance, we begin to understand the vital connection between the past, the present, and the future, as well as the significance of the "passage," the "threshold," and the "door" itself. The door or gate symbolizes moving from one plane of understanding or awareness to another—emotionally, intellectually, or spiritually. The door that leads to the future may sometimes signify the unknown or the untried. When we actually pass through that door, we may discover the familiar, clearly connected to where we've been before, and our transition from present to future will appear seamless and orderly. At other times, though, passing through the door to the future entails taking risks and letting go of pieces of the past and present. These are the transitions that are fraught—when we have had to close doors behind us to move forward or when someone else has closed a door for us and we must find a new entrance to the future. Even so, Jana reminds us that the way into our future is always lit by the wisdom we have gleaned from the past and that the open door represents opportunity. As Helen Keller wrote, "When one door of happiness closes, another opens; but often we look so long at the closed door that we do not see the one which has been opened for us." Jana helps us keep our eyes on the open door.

With Jana by your side, you can begin to explore your future by first gaining a better understanding of your past and your present. Use your journal writing to make connections among the turning points in your life, and see if a pattern emerges that links where you have been, where you find yourself now, and where you would like to go. You can also draw your own "life map" as a way of coming to the same understanding. Tape pieces of paper together and draw a map of your life's pathway. Don't render it as a straight road or highway, but incorporate forks, turns, and even dead ends. A fork can signify an important choice you made or a defining event, while a turn can stand for a choice that led your life in a new direction. Dead ends can stand for choices or events you now acknowledge to have been failures or mistakes. Use this graphic representation to better understand the relationship among the different decades or periods of your life. Adding dates and names to the map, along with descriptions of how you felt at the time, can be valuable.

Alternatively, you can create an altar to Jana out of objects you associate with the most important events of your life, past and present. Use photographs and write descriptions on cards to serve as visual markers of your personal journey. Create a path on your altar to symbolize the future; you can make it out of pebbles, beads, shells, or even dried beans. Once again, your goal is to come to a greater understanding of the links among the moments, events, and relationships in your life so that you can move into the future with an open mind and heart.

Gratitude
Flora

Petals were everywhere—along with lovemaking, courtesans, music, and dance—during the Roman festival dedicated to Flora, the goddess of the flowers; this springtime celebration heralded the gifts of blossom, bloom, and the season of renewal. While the Greeks had envisioned the same goddess in a more demure aspect, naming her Chloris or "greening," the Romans' festival was a joyous "thank-you" in which participants enjoyed demonstrating their honor and gratitude. In Botticelli's painting *Primavera* or "Spring," the chaste Chloris is transformed by Zephyr, the winds of passion, into the lush, sensual Flora bedecked with flowers.

Flora is the guardian of gratitude, reminding us that gratitude shouldn't be a superficial response based on piety or good manners but should rise from deep within us as we experience a heightened awareness of all the gifts of life. This isn't the "thank-you" we murmur automatically on cue but a swelling up of feeling as we open our bodies and souls to the small details and grand gestures that make life joyous and fulfilling. Both sense and spirit participate in true gratitude, which moves us in both literal and metaphorical ways.

Flora's essence is the flower, the universal emblem of beauty, transcendence, tribute, and thanks. Bringing flowers into our daily lives both stimulates and expresses gratitude, since flowers have long been left as gifts of thanks and remembrance on altars and shrines. If you garden, you may want to plant a small bed of gratitude, using symbolism to inform your choices. Or you can bring single blossoms or a bouquet indoors as an evocation of Flora's spirit. Following are just a few of the flowers that carry meaning and significance:

The Chrysanthemum: A solar emblem in the Far East as well as a symbol of unity, cohesion, and completeness, the chrysanthemum is associated with joy. As a fall flower, it reminds us of the gifts of each season in kind.

The Daisy: Symbol of innocence and the refreshed spirit (this flower closes up at night and opens again in the morning to reveal its yellow center, or "day's eye"), the daisy is associated with childhood and simplicity.

The Iris: Named after the Greek goddess of the rainbow, this flower signifies union as well as reconciliation; its simple beauty makes it perfect for a meditation of thanks.

The Lily: Sacred to many goddesses and thus an emblem of the feminine as well as purity, the lily's shape, color, and scent make it a powerful emblem of the gifts of the earth.

The Lotus: The sacred flower of Buddhism and Hinduism, it signifies spiritual emergence. While not an indoor flower, it can be used to great effect in a water garden.

The Orchid: Rare and often costly, this flower is an emblem of purity and spiritual perfection; it can represent our aspirations and hopes.

The Rose: The queen of flowers in Western tradition, the rose has as many meanings as it has petals—all of them positive and uplifting. It was the sacred flower of Aphrodite, the Greek goddess of love, as well as of the Virgin Mary, who was herself named the "Mystical Rose." Emblem of the body and the soul, it symbolizes beauty and rebirth.

The Sunflower: Native to the Americas, it signifies emergence and continuing fruitfulness—the seed gives forth the magnificent head, which yields more seeds in turn—and the power of the sun. What better expression of joy than the sunflower, indoors or out?

Flora's spirit can also be invoked in winter by forcing bulbs or with bowls of scented potpourri. Remember that gratitude can become a daily expression for you and your family when you enact simple rituals, such as saying grace or recounting blessings at week's end.

Healing
Hygeia

The guardian of healing the body and the psyche is Hygeia, daughter of the Greek god of medicine, Asclepius. Worship of the goddess—whose name yields our word *hygiene*—spread through Greece after Athens was devastated by a plague in the fifth century BCE. The Romans also venerated her as Salus. She is usually depicted as a beautiful young woman, with a snake wrapped around her body or feeding from her hand. Her connection to the snake—snakes were kept in her temples, where women left locks of their hair as an offering for invocations of health—is a key to her nature. A staff with a snake wrapped around it—a caduceus—was the attribute of both Hygeia and Asclepius, and still represents the medical profession today.

From the Neolithic Era onward, the snake was connected to the divine energy of the feminine life force and to the ancient goddesses; the snake's ability to shed its skin and thus be "reborn" made it a potent emblem of regeneration. The serpent's movement—meandering, turning, twisting, flowing—echoed the movement of life-giving water, and thus serpentine patterns summoned both the feminine waters and the snake. For thousands of years, the snake and the divine feminine were connected; the Egyptian goddess Isis was pictured wearing a crown of snakes, while Cretan statues from 1600 BCE portray goddesses or priestesses with snakes wound around their bodies. A gilt and bronze statue of Athena, found on the Acropolis, shows coiling snakes on her clothing. These images connect Hygeia to the Great Mother herself—the energy of the feminine in the universe—and make her part of a healing whole.

Healing, after all, means to "make whole." Hygeia reminds us that to heal ourselves we must first liberate and nurture the feminine force within so that we can summon our own divine energy. She reminds us that oneness of body and spirit is a prerequisite to true health or wholeness. Her attribute, the snake, teaches us that the possibility of transformation and rebirth—of body and soul—is ours to claim.

Build an altar to Hygeia to confirm your commitment to healing. Images of snakes as well as those associated with water—fish, water lilies, or frogs, for example—exemplify rebirth. Use objects that signify wholeness—

things uncut or unbruised, such as fruits or flowers or even unburned candles—on the altar, as well as symbols of the divine feminine.

Among the books that can help you as you fully embrace the spirit of Hygeia are Dr. Rachel Naomi Remen's *Kitchen Table Wisdom: Stories That Heal*, Dr. Herbert Benson's *Timeless Healing: The Power of Biology and Belief*, and Dr. Bernie S. Siegel's *Love, Medicine, and Miracles*.

Illumination
Amaterasu Omikami

Chief among the Shinto *kami,* or spirits, Amaterasu is the goddess of the sun (her name means "Heavenly Shining Deity"), whose shrine at Ise is Japan's most sacred place. Daughter of the god Izanagi, she had two brothers, Tsukiyomi-no-Mikoto, the moon god, and Susano-Wo, the storm god. The three siblings ascended to the heavens together, where Susano-Wo wreaked such havoc—he smashed everything in sight in a drunken rage after realizing his sister was more powerful than he—that Amaterasu fled the heavenly precincts and took refuge in a cave. All the light in the world disappeared, turning the earth so barren that even the rice died. All the deities tried to lure Amaterasu from the cave with all manner of blandishments, including music, laughter, and dancing—but to no avail. Finally, in desperation, they held a mirror up to the mouth of the cave, and as the now curious Amaterasu peeked out, she could see her own glorious beauty for the first time. As she stood entranced by the reflection, the gods closed the cave behind her—and thus Amaterasu's light returned to the world.

The mirror into which Amaterasu's light shines symbolizes the purity of the enlightened soul as well as the illumination that follows from full and conscious self-reflection. While the story of Amaterasu is, on one level, a myth about the seasons and the sun's withdrawal from the winter skies, it also describes the soul in hiding, shut off from growth and possibility. We can also understand the story as a parable about the need for emergence, and a warning about what can happen to the "light" within us if we don't give voice to all the parts of the self that need articulation.

Shintoism isn't, as Joseph Campbell explained, "the following of some set-down moral code, but a living in gratitude and awe of the mystery of things." The story of Amaterasu and her mirror reminds us that illumination can be sought both near and far; we may find knowledge in books and teachings, or in a sun-drenched meadow. Just as her mirror reflects her inner purity, so too we can look into our own souls for a reflection of the awe and mystery of all things.

Amaterasu guards our highest aspirations, our yearning for spiritual direction and definition, and our desire to invite the sacred into our daily lives. She reminds us that truth can be found in many places, beginning within. She is the sun that rises on the new day, offering us possibility; her daily return reminds us that the journey of spirit is ongoing, and that the new light of morning brings fresh answers to old questions.

The American writer Edith Wharton once wrote, "There are two ways of spreading light: to be the candle or the mirror that reflects it." Invite Amaterasu's spirit into your life by welcoming her each morning; celebrate her company each night by lighting candles to illuminate whatever darkness remains within.

Pleasure
The Cat

In the warmth of the afternoon, she lies with her supple body and limbs fully stretched out on the floor, the sunlight dappling her fur, warming her skin. Her breathing is soft and rhythmic, undisturbed. Later, curled in a lap, she settles in, taking her time until she's fully comfortable; then she closes her eyes and gives herself over to purring. Sensual, she grooms herself carefully and slowly; is it the act of cleaning herself that pleases her or the feeling of her rough tongue on her skin and fur? Her world is defined by pleasures, large and small—her favored perch for sunning, the warm spot on the bed, the taste of a dollop of yogurt or a sliver of meat, the best place for dreaming of birds and butterflies. Never languid, she always moves with feminine grace—providing us a feline mirror in which to glimpse a self without worry, receptive to all the universe offers in the way of smell, taste, touch, sight, sound.

It's little wonder that the cat goddess of the Egyptians, Bast, was a benign and caring guardian of life and its pleasures. If Sekmet, the lion-headed goddess, symbolized the brutal and destructive aspect of the sun, Bast represented the sun's gentle warmth—its rays releasing the sweet smells of the earth in flower, green and loamy. She was the "Lady of the East," place of the rising sun and thus of hope, possibility, birth, and rebirth. Bast may first have been worshipped as a cat and later as a cat-headed goddess, or perhaps she was always pictured in both forms. We know that cats were highly honored in Egypt, their bodies mummified and buried with great ceremony. Statues celebrate Bast in her different guises; one shows her as a regal cat with fine and pointed features, an earring in one ear, and, around her neck the wedjat eye, or the Eye of Horus, signifying healing and protection. Another shows her standing with a sistrum—symbolic of pleasure and desire—in one hand and an aegis with a cat's head in the other. She is also a protector because small kittens sit at her feet. As recorded by Herodotus, the festivities dedicated to Bast were days long and filled with pleasure; they were attended by hundreds of thousands of celebrants who came singing and dancing, playing the sistrum and flute, merrymaking, and drinking more wine than was consumed all the rest of the year. Bast's temple and its setting were beautiful, and the festival celebrated the open and free exploration of the senses.

In our busy and sometimes complicated lives, it becomes too easy to forget what gives us pleasure and how we feel when our senses and our bodies are stimulated. The woman in the business suit commuting to work or the woman in jeans and a tee shirt sitting in an idling car waiting for the kids to get out of school is still a sensual creature who thrives on touch, sound, smell, taste, and sight. Take time for yourself, Cat whispers, pleasure your senses. Don't forget to nourish your spirit with touch, sound, smell, taste, and sight. Allow yourself the time and space for all your desires to be awakened; let yourself be demanding and ask for what you need. The routines of adult life, the responsibilities of work, and especially those of motherhood—not to mention the number of hours we've been up by the time we actually get to bed—can be deadening for the cat in all of us, and it's important to keep her part and parcel of the women we are. We often deny our own appetites without thinking—because we're too tired, too stressed, too played out at the end of the day.

The cat is the guardian of our pleasures and our appetites. Invite her back into your life by remembering your own sensual needs in whatever way you wish. The poet Edna St. Vincent Millay, a woman of great sensuality and appetite, perhaps expressed it best in her poem "Feast":

> I drank at every vine.
>> The last was like the first.
> I came upon no wine
>> So wonderful as thirst.
>
> I gnawed at every root.
>> I ate of every plant.
> I came upon no fruit
>> So wonderful as want.

Renewal
The Deer

To come upon the stag or doe in the woods or forest is a crystallizing moment: in the dappled sunlight, this graceful and gentle creature seems to blend in seamlessly with its surroundings, standing silent and stock-still, its wide and luminous eyes focused on the perceived intruder. In an instant, the deer is nothing less than fluid motion, moving quickly through the trees with the rustle of fallen leaves and branches trailing behind it like an echo.

The deer has long been considered a sacred animal in many parts of the world, whether as companion to the Greek huntress Artemis or as herald of daybreak to the Pawnees. The stag's magnificent antlers—shed and then regrown—symbolized fecundity and the sun, as well as the cycle of rebirth and renewal; their shape recalled the Tree of Life, its roots reaching deep into the earth and its branches arcing skyward. The stag was a spirit guide that could link heaven and earth and help seekers find the true path. In Norse legend, four stags grazed in the top branches of Yggdrasill, the world tree, creating the passage of time; they ate buds (hours), blossoms (days), and branches (seasons). The deer—whether a stag or a doe—was overall a symbol of gentleness and spirit. Its ability to find and drink from fresh-flowing streams—its sure-footedness on rocks and stones—became a powerful metaphor for faith and spirit, echoed in the words of the Forty-second Psalm, "As the hart panteth after the water brooks, so panteth my soul after Thee, O God."

Deer can guide us when our bodies and spirits feel worn and tired, when our paths have become tiresome grooves, when we thirst for new meaning and knowledge. We can call upon her energy and fleetness to get us out of the rut we're in, and her ability to find fresh streams to inspire and invigorate us. Her beauty and gentle grace remind us to open our eyes to the beauty and grace of the world around us.

There is a wonderful and inspiring *Jataka,* or "birth story," of the Buddha featuring a deer hero. There are 547 such stories, each of which demonstrates the law of karma, that the acts of a previous life affect the current one. In this particular *Jataka,* the Banyan Deer is one of the Buddha's previous incarnations. This story can serve as the beginning of a meditation or simply inspire us as we search for ways of renewing ourselves.

A golden stag with eyes like jewels, silver antlers, and hooves of diamonds was king of a herd of five hundred, which were known as the Banyan Deer. Nearby, another equally glorious stag king ruled over an equally large herd known as the Branch Deer. The country they lived in was ruled by a king who lived to hunt and eat venison. Never content to hunt alone, the king required all the towns-people to accompany him on the hunt each day. Their work and their fields lay neglected. Finally, the people decided to build a deer park for the king so that he could hunt to his heart's content and they could tend to their lives. They built a beautiful enclosure, within which lived the two herds of Banyan and Branch Deer.

When the king saw the regal and stately stag kings, he immediately granted them their lives. But the rest of their herds still fled with fear whenever the king or his servant entered the park to collect the daily meal. The deer would try to run and hide, but it was impossible; each day, even though the king needed only one deer, many were hurt and maimed in the melee caused by the king's arrows.

The Banyan King called for the Branch King and asked him to consider a proposition. Rather than let so many die, one deer each day would sacrifice itself for the herd, laying its head on a chopping block, thus sparing the others' suffering. And so it went.

But one day, the turn fell to a Branch doe who had just given birth. She begged the Branch King for mercy since her fawn would die without her. The Branch King refused, saying that the rules were inviolate. Desperate, she turned to the Banyan King, who immediately offered to give his life for hers.

That day, the king's servant entered the park and saw the golden stag with his head on the block. Knowing that the stag was never to be killed, he went to get the king. The puzzled king asked the Banyan deer why he was there.

The Banyan King replied that he was willing to die for the sake of the doe and her fawn, whereupon the king, moved by his decision, granted the Banyan King and all the other deer mercy, giving up the hunt for good. But not until the king promised to give up hunting all creatures— from the four-footed mammals to the fish in the waters to the birds in the sky—did the golden stag finally raise his head from the chopping block and get to his feet.

While this Buddhist story teaches the greatness of compassion and the power of its recognition, it also details how old ways of doing things can be abandoned and new paths sought—by the townspeople, the Banyan King, and, finally, the earthly king himself. This sacred fable serves to remind us that renewing our lives and spirits can be accomplished by active choice—by letting go of worn-out ways of looking at and thinking about life and its challenges. The king, after all, never regrets giving up the hunt or his venison, not for a moment; he has opened himself up to new understanding after seeing generosity and compassion incarnate.

Let Deer's example invigorate you as you search for new answers. Renewal, after all, must come from within.

Simplicity
Saint Thérèse of Lisieux

Her life was short—she succumbed to tuberculosis at the age of twenty-four—but her inspirational legacy, captured in her autobiography, *The Story of a Soul*, has made her a presence in the lives of many women, including those raised outside of the Catholic faith. The youngest of nine children, only five of whom would reach adulthood, she was born in 1873 in Alençon, France, as Thérèse Martin. Her mother died when she was four, and her father and older siblings coddled and protected her as the baby of the family. She experienced a conversion at the age of fourteen and, a year later, committed herself to lead a devoted life of prayer in a Carmelite convent. She lived there until her death nine years later.

Her autobiography—begun when her prioress asked that she describe her childhood, and published after her death in 1899—is an examination of faith and the way of grace. Is it possible, Thérèse asked, that only the great are granted grace? Her answer was rooted in her ability to see the brushstrokes of a divine painter in the ordinary detail of the world: "I can still feel the deep and poetic impression which the wheat fields made on me when I saw them all studded with poppies and cornflowers and daisies. Even then I loved far distances, wide space, and the trees. The whole of nature, in fact, enchanted me and raised my soul toward Heaven." Indeed, the very variety of the world seemed to her to indicate a master hand at work making a place for "the splendor of the rose" and the "lily's whiteness," as well as the scent of the violet and the daisy's charms. So too, in the world of souls, there was room for the great as well as the "little flowers," among whom she counted herself. Thérèse's credo of simple faith—of finding grace in the ordinary—has much to teach us.

In the busy lives we lead, simplicity too often seems the one thing that eludes us, buried beneath the inevitable clutter of mail and laundry at week's end. In *A Gift from the Sea*, Anne Morrow Lindbergh—herself a wife, mother to five, sister, daughter, and writer—aptly describes the "centrifugal force" that seems to dominate many a woman's life: "To ask how little, not how much, can I get along with. To say—is it necessary?—when I am tempted to add one more accumulation to my life, when I am pulled toward one more centrifugal activity."

Lindbergh's question—"Is it necessary?"—runs counter to much of what we've been taught, what the world around us declares again and again. If dessert is good, we're bred to ask for seconds. While one job offer is good, we all know that two job offers are better—even though we can be in only one place at a time. If we find one object we love, our impulse is to find another just like it so that we eventually end up with a shelf or a drawer full. From childhood on, we hear that more is always better, and inevitably, we pass this message on to our children. All of us have been raised to be collectors of people, successes, talents, and experiences—and it makes us unhappy when we end up with fewer than we expected. We are taught to look at the big picture, but along the way, a great many of us forget that the picture is in the details.

Cutting back on our commitments is one way to simplify—that's the answer to "Is it necessary?"—as is buying less or cleaning out our closets more often. But, in addition, we have to permit ourselves the space and time to see dignity, grace, and beauty in the ordinary things of life. After we've created a sense of spaciousness in our lives by cutting back, we have to allow ourselves to look into the heart of things. This isn't about auster-ity or self-abnegation—you don't have to throw out the fifty pairs of shoes in your closet, if you have them, or get rid of your collectibles—but about a shift in attitude. Teach yourself to take in the details, and as you become more observant, you will find great joy in simple things.

Invoke Thérèse, and put a single flower in a vase—it can be her rose, if you want—and observe it, separated from the profusion of the bouquet. Spend time really looking at the objects you own and love to rediscover their beauty—detail by detail. Spend time with those you love, and really listen; open yourself to the sound of laughter, the beauty of a smile. Be content and grateful for what you do have without longing for what you don't.

At the end of every week, make a list of all the things in this life that make you happy, joyous, and comfortable; begin each new month by reading these lists to yourself and offer a prayer of thanks.

My own list would begin like this:

1. My daughter's face, especially first thing in the morning.
2. The man I love, the sound of his laughter, the gift of his touch.
3. The beauty of words on the page.
4. The sun on my face.

Solace
Demeter

For the ancient Greeks, it was the great sorrow of this preeminent goddess of the earth which first came to mind. They knew how she had wandered the earth, searching for her only daughter, for nine days and nights with only a torch to light the way. Her daughter, Persephone, had been abducted from the verdant fields of the land of the living and raped by the god of the underworld, Pluto. No one—neither god nor mortal—offered Demeter help. Finally, on the tenth day, Helios, the god of the sun, and Hecate, queen of the night, told her what had happened.

Furious at the betrayal, Demeter stormed from Olympus, home to the gods and goddesses, and wandered the earth, disguised as a mortal. She met two young women who brought the goddess to their mother, Metaneira. Metaneira had borne a much longed-for son late in life, and invited Demeter to be the boy's nurse. Her maternal instincts reawakened, Demeter fed the boy ambrosia, food of the gods, and each night placed him in the fire so that he would become immortal. Metaneira became curious and distrustful of how her son was flourishing and began to spy on Demeter. One night, the horrified mother saw Demeter putting her son into the fire. Confronted, Demeter revealed herself and instructed the people of Eleusis—it means "the place of happy arrival"—to build her a temple.

The temple built, Demeter retired to its precincts, keening and mourning her only child. Inconsolable, she withdrew her gifts from the earth. The vegetation withered, the animals starved, and the offerings to the gods ceased; the din of mourning filled the air. At this moment of crisis, Zeus, chief among the gods, finally agreed to hear Demeter's complaints. Uncompromising, the goddess demanded her daughter's release. Ruling against his brother Pluto, Zeus agreed to return Persephone to earth provided she had eaten nothing in the underworld. Pluto, though, had tricked the girl into eating the single seed of a pomegranate, and thus Zeus decreed that Persephone would spend one-third of the year in the underworld and two-thirds of the year on earth in Demeter's company.

Many of us first encounter the story of Demeter and Persephone in children's collections of myths, where it is usually explained as a simple tale about the changing seasons or the rebirth of the moon in the night sky. But when it was still a sacred story, it was the basis for the most profound of Greek rites, the Eleusinian Mysteries. Because the essence of these ceremonies was kept secret, known only to the priests and initiates, its details remain unknown. But we do know that the ceremonies revolved around a sacred, transformative revelation, of which the dramatist Sophocles wrote, "Thrice-blessed are those mortals who have seen these rites and thus enter into Hades: for them alone there is life, for all others all is misery."

In the broadest sense, the Greeks understood Demeter's lesson to be one of hope and solace, evoking a profound and sublime belief in the continuum of pain and pleasure, loss and gain, dark and light, death and life. The three-part ceremony at Eleusis demonstrated to the initiates that life and death, gain and loss, pleasure and sorrow were not eternally opposed states but were inextricably linked to each other.

Demeter's sacred story still has resonance for us today. Anne Baring and Jules Cashford point out that Demeter's story is inseparable from that of her daughter, who is sometimes known simply as Kore, meaning "maiden" or perhaps "sprout." Persephone is the seed that falls from the ripe grain—seeming lifeless when it is swallowed up by the dark earth—only to emerge from the ground as new growth. It suggests that each loss we experience is, in fact, a new beginning and that life can only emerge from both love and loss.

This ancient lesson about the nature of solace is echoed in contemporary wisdom as well. In Pema Chödrön's wonderful book *When Things Fall Apart: Heart Advice for Difficult Times*, the Buddhist perspective yields a similar vision; she writes: "Only to the extent that we expose ourselves over and over to annihilation can that which is indestructible be found in us."

Demeter's story also reminds us that solace is a destination requiring a long journey—a journey through dark places with little light to guide us, through anger and mourning, through tears and cries. It may be a lonely journey, and it may seem that no one else can feel what you are feeling. But Demeter teaches that, with effort and understanding, we can get to where healing begins.

Build an altar to solace with objects that resonate with the love or connection you are mourning. Put flowers on the altar and permit them to wither and go to seed so that you can witness the larger cycle of life. Plant seeds or a flowering bulb in a small pot to help you visualize the reemergence of the life force.

Spirituality
Mary Magdalene

She is the guardian of spirituality because her story, like so many of those pertaining to the divine feminine, reminds us that the journey of spirit is sometimes an act of reclamation and recovery, in which we rescue what has been covered up from the patriarchal past, and bring its truth and illumination to bear on the present. What we know about Mary Magdalene asserts—this time through the prism of the early Christian tradition—that the spirit of the Christian faith didn't always devalue the body or the feminine.

As happened to the goddesses before her, what was once Mary Magdalene's especial, favored status became fully negated over time. Described in the New Testament as the first witness to the resurrected Christ in the Garden of Gethsemane, and described in the Gnostic Gospels as a priestess and acolyte, Mary Magdalene became known over time as the penitent whore. The change was so complete that institutions claiming to rehabilitate "fallen women"—prostitutes and unwed mothers—became known as "Magdalenes" in the United States and England. The familiar depiction of her at the cross, her face streaked with tears, became synonymous with cheap or "maudlin" sentiment.

Yet the woman revealed in the New Testament is a woman unafraid of looking into the heart of things; she expresses herself with physical gestures—she cries, she kneels, she touches. The Gospel traditionally ascribed to John describes Mary Magdalene moving toward the risen Jesus to embrace him—only to be told "Touch Me Not." She, not Jesus's mother, is the only female eyewitness to the central mystery of the Christian faith, the Resurrection; she is distinguished not only by her gender, but by the nature of her belief. Unlike Jesus's male followers, she needs no tactile proof to believe what she has seen; she is persuaded by the sound of Christ's voice alone.

The Gnostics—losers in the battle for theological control of the Christian Church—saw Mary Magdalene as the embodiment of the feminine wisdom and spirit (Sophia) that animated the universe. Two of the surviving Gnostic texts—suppressed since the second century CE and only accidentally rediscovered in the middle of the twentieth century—reveal Mary Magdalene in other aspects. In "The Gnostic Gospel of Mary," the ascended

Christ appears to Mary Magdalene—not to Peter, who objects as vigorously and jealously as a spurned schoolboy—and instructs her on how to direct his ministry. "The Gnostic Gospel of Philip" paints the loving relationship between Christ and Mary Magdalene as intimate and physical. She was called Jesus's "companion."

History belongs to the victors, and by the time the New Testament writings now known as Timothy and Acts were completed, Mary Magdalene was no longer counted among the apostles, who became an all-male band of twelve. When the resurrected Christ's appearances are catalogued in Acts, his appearance to Mary Magdalene in the garden isn't even mentioned. Yet we know that for centuries she was called "The Apostle of the Apostles" and she "Who Knew All." In the early years of the first millennium after Christ, Mary Magdalene was the Christian successor to the ancient priestesses, oracles, and sibyls who preceded her. Long before her name conjured up the repentant sinner, she answered prayers and devotions as one of Jesus's true followers.

Mary Magdalene the sinner is the bookend to the other Mary, Jesus's mother; the dualism of the two Marys—one the whore, the other the virgin inviolate—became the either/or standard for women that animated the Christian tradition and, by extension, became part of the vocabulary of the secular West. As such, Mary Magdalene is part of the backdrop of many cultural archetypes and mythologies pertaining to women. She became, in time, the "Whore with the Heart of Gold"—think Julia Roberts in *Pretty Woman*—beloved of Hollywood. Even her "maudlin" behavior informs society's idea of what is feminine (weak and sentimental) and masculine (strong and tearless).

But for those of us who are seeking a spirituality that will reflect our female identity—as Patricia Lynn Reilly phrased it so eloquently in the title of her book *A God Who Looks Like Me*—Mary Magdalene represents a spiritual history that can be reclaimed for the present and can restore wholeness to the divine feminine. Mary Magdalene is the only one of Jesus's followers mentioned in the Gospels who isn't described as someone's wife or mother. This may signal her independence, but it may equally reflect that her own status or that of her husband was so important that she needed no identification. Instead, she belonged only to the place she was born, a town called Magdala, meaning "tower," "high place," or, alternatively, "great."

Images of towers and cities once crowned the ancient goddesses, and the most holy places of the ancient religions were peaks and mountains; by her name, Mary of Magdala is located within that tradition. She teaches us that, in search of the spirit, we can lay claim to a vision of the feminine in which body and soul are united within the divine.

Invite spirit into your life by honoring the feminine within you. Become more conscious of the harsh standards of beauty and perfection our society imposes on girls and women, and work on letting go of them. Loving yourself is the first step toward opening up the soul. Rediscover the feminine spirit through books such as Susan Haskins's *Mary Magdalene: Myth and Metaphor* or Patricia Lynn Reilly's *A God Who Looks Like Me.*

Vision

Fortuna

Long before she became known as "Lady Luck" and was pictured wearing a blindfold and holding the wheel of chance, Fortuna, the Roman goddess of destiny, inspired sacred shrines that were visited by all, but particularly women. Only a single aspect of Fortuna, Fors Fortuna, was associated with what we call "luck." Instead, she was a guardian goddess, pictured with a cornucopia—symbolic of abundance, prosperity, and divine generosity—in one hand and a ship's rudder, signifying direction, in the other. Her domain encompassed the fruits of life, literally and metaphorically, as well as directional guidance, and her primary sanctuaries at Antium and Praeneste were oracular, places of vision and guidance. At Praeneste, her oracle was called Fortuna Primigenia—the "first-born"—and there she was the guardian of expectant women and mothers. Elsewhere, she was worshipped in many aspects. As Fortuna Virginesis, she was the protector of newly married women; as Fortuna Virilis, she helped women preserve their husbands' love; as Fortuna Redux, she was that "which leads or brings back"; as Fortuna Gubernans, she was the helmsperson setting the direction of life. Overall, she was Fortuna Muliebris, "belonging to women," and what she promised was good fortune, Fortuna Bona, both material and spiritual.

Later, in patriarchal hands, she became chance personified as a fickle woman, but it seems likely that she was once a guardian of difficult transitions and changes, representing destiny as a combination of both that which can't be changed or controlled and that which can be altered through individual thought, action, and demeanor. Perhaps the best analogy we have in modern times are the often-quoted words of the Serenity Prayer:

> God, grant me the serenity to accept the things I
> cannot change, the courage to change the things
> I can, and the wisdom to know the difference.

As a guardian, Fortuna can help us understand the very distinctions this prayer addresses: she encourages us to accept the fixed aspects of our lives with equanimity and grace; to confront those things we can affect and govern; and to distinguish among them so that we can use our energy, talents, and devotion wisely. She thus becomes, as she was for Roman women, a guardian of true vision—helping us to assess what we need to look at realistically, on the one hand, and supporting us in maintaining the vision and conviction of our dreams, on the other. She teaches us to stop railing at the things that are beyond our control but that sap our energy and limit our views of ourselves and our future nonetheless. Our complaints take on many forms—the supportive family we didn't have, the break we didn't get, the job we didn't land, the person who betrayed our trust, the decision made in haste or error—but Fortuna can help us see each for what it truly is. She allows us to recognize the dead ends in our lives—jobs, relationships, or emotional connections—that we cannot change and that are holding us back. She turns our attention to those things we can change for the better—bringing the gift of good fortune into our lives—and encourages us in our hopes, dreams, and ambitions.

Begin a visualization by imagining yourself as a sailor on a small sailboat with a single rudder. Try to envision the things you can't change, or that are beyond your control, as winds and weather—they may threaten to flood or sink the boat one moment, and they may make sailing pleasant at another. Then, imagine the things that help guide your course—let the stars and the moon symbolize qualities and abilities that can help you reach your destination. Finally, work on visualizing where you wish to land—the safe harbor and destination you are looking for. Visualize the coves and inlets you decide to pass by and see yourself sailing and sailing until you get where you need to go. And keep Fortuna, who holds both the cornucopia and the rudder in her hands, in mind.

Womanhood
Changing Woman

She is there when the definitions and demands of womanhood and all our feelings connected to them swirl around us, creating anxiety and confusion. A million questions and few answers: How can I be strong and caring? Can I balance my ambition with motherhood? Does my true womanhood emerge at work, in love, with children, in my community, with my friends, or alone? Does my womanhood depend on ovaries and breasts or does it reside elsewhere? Is womanhood biology or is it a state of mind? What kind of a woman am I or should I be? How does my womanhood separate me from or connect me to others? How do the cycles of my body affect the way I think and feel? How does my body—changing over time—reflect my sense of who I am?

The primordial goddess of Native America, Changing Woman is the guardian to whom we turn for support when the physical changes and life passages unique to women take center stage in our lives. She helps us when the cycles of our bodies feel more like a millstone than a blessing—when we have to bully our way through a busy day, even though we are bloated and cranky. She helps us honor our singular biology even when it disappoints us—when we have difficulty conceiving or carrying a child, or when pregnancy and birth leave us feeling a sense of desperate isolation instead of the rosy fulfillment we expected. She is there for us when we see that our faces and bodies bear the marks of experience and time in a culture that admires the young and the flawless, the face and body free of wrinkles and stretch marks. She guards us during the long years of perimenopause and through menopause—when some of us will feel at war with the bodies we inhabit. Most of all, she helps us see each and every change in our physical bodies as part of a continuum—a female prism through which the white light of life becomes an ever-changing spectrum of color.

Although she was also known as "White Painted Woman" or "White Shell Woman," Changing Woman's primary name—*Esta'anatlehi*—reflects her ability to recapitulate all the stages of a woman's natural life. While she ages into an old and feeble woman, she can also transform herself by walking through four rooms identified with the cardinal directions. The traditional associations with the directions are reversed in this sacred story:

Changing Woman visits the room of the east, associated with rebirth, and emerges only slightly younger, while she becomes a young girl in the north, traditionally associated with the death-like sleep of winter. This story suggests not only the rejuvenation of the earth, with which Changing Woman is identified, but the existence of an essential self that stays unchanging and is immune to the ravages of time. Young or old, she is still Changing Woman.

Sacred stories of the Navajo recount how the infant Changing Woman was found on a mountaintop, hidden by rain clouds. First Man and First Woman found her and fed her dew and pollen. The child thrived and grew ever lovelier. Changing Woman's menarche was marked by the first puberty ceremony and set the pattern for all such Navajo rituals. Woman's rites—at puberty, at marriage, and then again at the birth of a first child—invoked Changing Woman as the guardian and embodiment of growth. Other stories portrayed Changing Woman as both a founder and savior to the Navajo people: she consorted with the Sun and gave birth to twin monster slayers who saved the world.

The rituals dedicated to Changing Woman make us more fully aware that our own culture does little or nothing to mark the passages of a woman's life from menarche to motherhood to menopause, and that we need to put these changes into a context of meaning by ourselves. Use Changing Woman as an inspiration to honor your own body and to explore your feelings about your womanly self. Becoming conscious of the passages in our lives strengthens us—and allows us to endow them with personal meaning. If you are the mother of a daughter, write a journal entry detailing how you felt when your child's body first became that of a young woman; bringing yourself back to that moment in time can help create a link between that younger self and the woman you are now. Use your journal to explore other passages—both positive and negative—that affected your sense of yourself as a woman. You might write about the first time you experienced true sexual fulfillment, for example, or your first pregnancy. Acknowledging these passages in writing will permit you to explore the connections among them.

As inspiration, keep in mind the beautiful Hopi poem entitled "Woman's Prayer to the Rising Sun for a Newborn Girl":

> Your beautiful rays may they color our faces;
> Being dyed in them, sometime at an old age
> We shall fall asleep old women.

✌ ACKNOWLEDGMENTS ✌

One of the things I really like about writing books is that, each time, I learn new things and meet new people. Paradoxically, while writing is essentially a solitary activity, it does always connect me to the larger world.

Especial thanks to Karen Bouris, publisher at Inner Ocean, for liking the idea, and then coming up with ideas to improve it. And kudos to Alma Bune.

I am grateful, too, for the support, help, and stories I received from old friends and their friends. Many *merci*'s, in alphabetical order, to Nancy Blair, the Goddess Incarnate; Connie Fails, Little Rock gal pal; Luisa Frey-Gaynor, for sharing her story; Diane Garisto, my good luck charm; Leslie Garisto, good friend and fellow scribe; Peter Israel, for the usual sundry good deeds; Claudia Karabaic Sargent, my friend and supporter and one of the finest people and Scorpios I know; Debby Coates; and Lori Stein, for generally being there and the treat of the occasional slice.

And then a big *merci* to two special people: Alexandra, for making my life as a mother a pleasure, and Craig, for finding the way back after thirty-five years.

❖ BIBLIOGRAPHY ❖

★★ indicates recommended reading

Allen, Paula Gunn. *The Sacred Hoop: Recovering the Feminine in American Indian Traditions*. Boston: Beacon Press, 1992. ★★

Barber, Elizabeth Wayland. *Women's Work: The First 20,000 Years*. New York: W. W. Norton, 1994.

Baring, Anne, and Jules Cashford. *The Myth of the Goddess: Evolution of an Image*. London and New York: Viking Arkana, 1991. ★★

Benson, Herbert, M.D. *Timeless Healing: The Power and Biology of Belief*. New York: Simon & Schuster, 1996. ★★

Bergman, Deborah. *The Knitting Goddess: Finding the Heart and Soul of Knitting through Instruction, Projects, and Stories*. New York: Hyperion, 2002. ★★

Biedermann, Hans. Translated by James Hulbert. *Dictionary of Symbolism*. New York: Facts on File, 1992.

Blair, Nancy. *Goddess Days: 365 Daily Meditations*. Gloucester, MA: Fair Winds Press, 2002. ★★

Bowker, John, ed. *The Oxford Dictionary of World Religions*. Oxford and New York: Oxford University Press, 1997.

Budge, E. A. Wallace. *The Gods of the Egyptians*. 2 vols. Reprint. New York: Dover Publications, 1969.

Campbell, Joseph. *The Masks of God: Occidental Mythology*. New York: Penguin Books, 1964. ★★

_____. *The Masks of God: Oriental Mythology*. New York: Penguin Books, 1962. ★★

_____. *The Masks of God: Primitive Mythology*. New York: Penguin Books, 1959. ★★

Chevalier, Jean, and Alain Gheerbrant. Translated by John Buchanan-Brown. *A Dictionary of Symbols*. New York: Penguin Books, 1996.

Chödrön, Pema. *When Things Fall Apart: Heart Advice for Difficult Times*. Boston: Shambala Publications, 2000. ★★

Cirlot, J. E. Translated by Jack Sage. *A Dictionary of Symbols*. New York: Philosophical Library, 1971.

Day, Michael, trans. *The Story of a Soul: The Autobiography of Saint Thérèsa of Lisieux*. Rockford, Illinois: Tan Books, 1997.

Davis-Kimball, Jeannine, with Mona Behan. *Warrior Women: An Archaeologist's Search for History's Hidden Heroines*. New York: Warner Books, 2002. ★★

Downing, Christine. *The Goddess: Mythological Images of the Feminine*. New York: Crossroads Publishing, 1981. ★★

Edwards, Carolyn McVickar. *The Storyteller's Goddess: Tales of the Goddess and Her Wisdom from around the World*. San Francisco: HarperSanFrancisco, 1991.

Estés, Clarissa Pinkola. *Women Who Run with the Wolves: Myths and Stories of the Wild Woman Archetype*. New York: Ballantine Books, 1997. ★★

Ferguson, George. *Signs and Symbols in Christian Art*. London: Oxford University Press, 1970.

Graves, Robert. *The Greek Myths*. 2 vols. New York: Penguin Books, 1990.

Hallam, Elizabeth. *Saints: Who They Are and How They Can Help You*. New York: Simon & Schuster, 1994.

Harvey, Paul. *The Oxford Companion to Classical Literature*. Oxford: Oxford University Press, 1937.

Haskins, Susan. *Mary Magdalene: Myth and Metaphor*. New York and San Diego: Harcourt Brace & Company, 1993. ★★

Johnson, Buffie. *Lady of the Beasts: Ancient Images of the Goddess and Her Sacred Animals*. San Francisco: Harper and Row, 1988.

Johnson, Thomas, ed. *The Complete Poems of Emily Dickinson*. Boston: Little, Brown, 1960.

Jordan, Michael. *Encyclopedia of Gods*. New York: Facts on File, 1993.

Kohn, Michael, trans. *The Shambala Dictionary of Buddhism and Zen*. Boston: Shambala Publications, 1991.

Larrington, Carolyne, ed. *The Feminist Companion to Mythology*. London: Pandora Press, 1992.

Latham, Edward Connery, ed. *The Poetry of Robert Frost.* New York: Holt, Rinehart and Winston, 1967.

Leach, Maria, ed. *Funk and Wagnalls Standard Dictionary of Folklore, Mythology, and Legend.* San Francisco: Harper & Row Publishers, 1984.

Lindbergh, Anne Morrow. *Gift from the Sea.* New York: Pantheon Books, 1975. ★★

Linn, Denise. *Sacred Space: Clearing and Enhancing the Energy of Your Home.* New York: Ballantine Books, 1995. ★★

Millay, Norma, ed. *Collected Poems: Edna St. Vincent Millay.* New York: Book-of-the-Month Club, 1990.

Neumann, Erich. *The Great Mother: An Analysis of the Archetype.* Translated by Ralph Manheim. Princeton: Princeton University Press, 1955. ★★

Pagels, Elaine. *The Gnostic Gospels.* New York: Vintage Press, 1979.

Pipher, Mary. *Reviving Ophelia: Saving the Selves of Adolescent Girls.* New York: Ballantine Books, 1994. ★★

Reichard, Gladys A. *Navaho Religion: A Study of Symbolism.* Princeton: Princeton University Press, 1977.

Reilly, Patricia Lynn. *A God Who Looks Like Me: Discovering a Woman-Affirming Spirituality.* New York: Ballantine Books, 1995. ★★

Remen, Rachel Naomi, M.D. *Kitchen Table Wisdom: Stories That Heal.* New York: Riverhead Books, 1996. ★★

Bibliography

Roberts, Elizabeth, and Elias Amidon, eds. *Life Prayers from Around the World: 365 Prayers, Blessings, and Affirmations to Celebrate The Human Journey.* San Francisco: HarperSanFrancisco, 1996.

Rossbach, Sarah. *Feng Shui: The Chinese Art of Placement.* New York: E. P. Dutton, 1983. ★★

Scully, Vincent. *The Earth, The Temple, and The Gods: Greek Sacred Architecture.* New York: Frederick A. Praeger, 1969.

Shepard, Paul, and Barry Sanders. *The Sacred Paw: The Bear in Nature, Myth, and Literature.* New York: Viking Press, 1985. ★★

Siegel, Bernie S., M.D. *Love, Medicine, and Miracles.* New York: Harper Perennial, 1986. ★★

Spear, William. *Feng Shui Made Easy: Designing Your Life with the Ancient Art of Placement.* San Francisco: HarperSanFrancisco, 1995. ★★

Steiger, Brad. *Totems: The Transformative Power of Your Personal Animal Totem.* San Francisco: HarperSanFrancisco, 1997.

Steinem, Gloria. *Revolution from Within.* Boston: Little, Brown, 1992. ★★

Stone, Merlin. *Ancient Mirrors of Womanhood: A Treasury of Goddess and Heroine Lore from around the World.* Boston: Beacon Press, 1990.

Streep, Peg. *Altars Made Easy: A Complete Guide to Creating Your Own Sacred Space.* San Francisco: HarperSanFrancisco, 1997.

_____. *Mary, Queen of Heaven: Miracles, Manifestations, and Meditations*. New York: Book of the Month Club, 1997.

_____. *Sanctuaries of the Goddess: The Sacred Landscapes and Objects*. Boston: Little, Brown, 1994.

Tresidder, Jack. *Dictionary of Symbols: An Illustrated Guide to Traditional Images, Icons, and Emblems*. San Francisco: Chronicle Books, 1997.

Walker, Barbara G. *The Woman's Encyclopedia of Myths and Secrets*. San Francisco: Harper & Row, 1983.

Warner, Marina. *Alone of All Her Sex: The Myth and Cult of the Virgin Mary*. New York: Vintage Books, 1983. ★★

_____. *Joan of Arc: The Image of Female Heroism*. Berkeley and Los Angeles: University of California Press, 1981. ★★

Williams, C. A. S. *Outlines of Chinese Symbolism and Art Motives*. New York: Dover Publications, 1976.

Wind, Edgar. *Pagan Mysteries in the Renaissance*. New York: W. W. Norton, 1968.

Winks, Cathy, and Anne Semans. *Sexy Mamas: Keeping Your Sex Life Alive While Raising Kids*. Maui, Hawaii: Inner Ocean Publishing, 2004. ★★

Woolger, Jennifer B., and Roger J. Woolger. *The Goddess Within: A Guide to the Eternal Myths That Shape Women's Lives*. New York: Ballantine Books, 1989.

Zimmer, Heinrich. Edited by Joseph Campbell. *Myths and Symbols in Indian Art and Civilisation*. New York: Harper Torchbooks, 1946.

∽: INDEX :∽

A

Acts, 215
Aesop, 42, 158
affirmation, 28
aging, 173-75
Aglaia, 87
Allen, Paula Gunn, 50
altars, 28-29
Amaterasu Omikami, 50, 193-95
Amazon, 99-102
Ammut, 11
Aphrodite, 61, 87-88, 128, 131-34, 188
Apollo, 61, 78, 103, 128
Ariadne, 73-76
Artemis, 32, 40, 101, 103-5, 200
Asclepius, 190
Athena, 50, 53-56, 191
Avalokiteshvara, 45

B

Banyan Deer, 201-2

Banyan King, 202-4
Barber, Elizabeth Wayland, 49, 168
Baring, Anne, 131, 211
Bast, 196-97
Bear, 147-50
Bee, 95-98
Benson, Herbert, 192
Bergman, Deborah, 51
Bird, 57-62
Blair, Nancy, 6
Botticelli, 186
Branch Deer, 202
Branch King, 202-3
Buddhism, 5, 45, 177, 201-4, 212
Butterfly, 106-9

C

Caesar, Augustus, 159
Campbell, Joseph, 194
Cashford, Jules, 131, 211
Castor, 153
Cat, 196-99

Çatal Hüyük, 40
Catholic Church, 93
Cerberus, 12
Changing Woman, 222-25
Charites, 87
Child, Julia, 79
Chloris, 186
Chödrön, Pema, 212
choice, 113-16
Christianity, 14, 106, 129,
    133, 139-40, 213-17
Chrysanthemum, 187
clarity, 37-39
commitment, 117-19
compassion, 120-23
confidence, 40-43
courage, 44-47
Crane, 173-75
creativity, 48-52
Cybele, 40, 95

D

Daisy, 187
Davis-Kimball, Jeannine, 101
Deer, 200-204
Demeter, 71, 95, 128, 153,
    209-12

Diana, 101, 182
Dickinson, Emily, 98
Dioscuri, 153
discipline, 53-56
divorce, 124-27
Dolphin, 128-30
Dove, 59
Dyad, 151-54

E

Eagle, 59-60
Eileithyia, 135
Eleusinian Mysteries, 211
energy, 176-78
Epona, 69-72
Eros, 128
Está anatlehi, 223
Estés, Clarissa Pinkola, 126
Euphrosyne, 87
exploration, 128-30
Eye of Horus, 197

F

Fates, 50
"Feast," 199
feng-huang, 57
Feng Shui Made Easy, 177

Feng Shui: The Chinese Art of Placement, 177
flexibility, 57-62
Flora, 186-89
flowers, 187-89
Fortuna, 218-21
Forty-second Psalm, 201
Frost, Robert, 115-16
fruitfulness, 179-81
future, 182-85

G

Gaia, 66-68, 78
Ganesh, 2, 9, 143-46
Gargareans, 100
Gemini, 153
gemstones, 68
generosity, 62-65
Gift from the Sea, 71, 206-7
Gnostic Gospels, 213-15
A God Who Looks Like Me, 216-17
Graces, 87-90, 133
Gratiae, 87
gratitude, 186-89
Graves, Robert, 101
The Great Mother, 180

Great White Horse of Uffington, 70
Green Tara, 5, 44-47
groundedness, 66-68
guardians
    choosing your own, 33
    learning from, 30-33
    representations of, 19
    space for, 18-21
    traditions, 10-14
    working with, 15-18, 29-32

H

Haskins, Susan, 217
healing, 190-92
Hecate, 113
Hera, 60, 135-38
Hermes, 128
Herodotus, 100, 197
Hestia, 32, 117-19
Hinduism, 1-2, 37, 95, 143, 176
Homer, 170
Homeric Hymn, 66
honey, 95-96
Hopi poem, 225

horses, 69-70
Horus, 82
Hygeia, 190-92

I
illumination, 193-95
Inanna, 6
independence, 69-72
ingenuity, 73-76
intellect, 77-79
intention, 80-83
intuition, 84-86
Iris, 161, 188
Isis, 80-83, 191
Izanagi, 193

J
Jana, 182-85
Janus, 13, 182
Jataka, 201
Jesus, 140, 213-17
Joan of Arc, 91-94
John, 214
journaling, 24-26
joy, 87-90
Judaism, 13-14
Juno, 13, 60

K
Kali, 6
kami, 193
Keller, Helen, 184
*Kitchen Table Wisdom: Stories
    That Heal*, 192
The Knitting Goddess, 51
Kore, 211
Kuan Yin, 9, 120-23

L
Ladon, 11
Lady Luck, 218
Lakshmi, 1-2, 62-65
La Pucelle, 91-94
Lares Familiares, 13
leadership, 91-94
Lilith, 6
Lily, 188
Lindbergh, Anne Morrow,
    71, 206-7
Linn, Denise, 177
Lioness, 40-43
Lotus, 64, 188
love, 131-34

Love, Medicine, and Miracles, 192

Luna, 84

M

Maat, 164–66

marriage, 135–38

Martin, Thérèse, 205

Mary Magdalene, 213–17

Mary Magdalene: Myth and Metaphor, 217

meditation, 21–22

Melissae, 95

Metaneira, 209

Metis, 53

Miao-Shan, 121

Millay, Edna St. Vincent, 199

minerals, 68

Minos, 74

Minotaur, 74

Moirai, 50

moon, 84–85, 95

Moses, Grandma, 79

Mother Earth, 66–68

motherhood, 139–42

The Myth of the Goddess: Evolution of an Image, 131

N

Native Americans, 13, 222–25

Navajo rituals, 224

negative imagery, 31–32

negotiation, 143–46

Neith, 49

Neumann, Erich, 180

New Testament, 140, 213–14

Nightingale, 60

Norns, 50

Norse legend, 12, 200

numen, 13

nurturance, 147–50

Nut, 179–81

O

Odin, 12

Odysseus, 167–69

The Odyssey, 167

O'Keeffe, Georgia, 51–52

Old Testament, 13–14, 161

oracle at Delphi, 78

Orchid, 188

Osiris, 81–82, 153

Owl, 54, 60

P

Panathenaea, 54

Parcae, 50

partnership, 151–54

Parvati, 144

Pasiphaë, 74

passion, 155–57

patience, 158–60

Peacock, 60–61

Pegasus, 70

Pele, 155–57

Penates, 13

Penelope, 167–70

peplos, 54

Persephone, 153, 209–11

Peter, 215

Philip, 215

phoenix, 57

Pipher, Mary, 102

platonic love, 133

pleasure, 196–99

Pluto, 209, 210

Pollux, 153

Porphyry, 95

Poseidon, 74, 128

prayer, 27–28

Pretty Woman, 216

Primavera, 186

productivity, 95–98

psyche, 106

R

Rainbow, 161–63

Re, 80, 95

reconciliation, 161–63

Reilly, Patricia Lynn, 216–17

Remen, Rachel Naomi, 192

renewal, 200–204

Resurrection of Christ, 214

Reviving Ophelia, 102

Revolution from Within, 102

Rhiannon, 58

Rig-Veda, 37

"The Road Not Taken,"
    115–16

Roberts, Julia, 216

Rose, 188

Rossbach, Sarah, 177

Rousseau, Henri, 86

S

*The Sacred Paw: The Bear in
    Nature, Myth, and
    Literature*, 147–48

Index

Sacred Space: Cleaning and Enhancing the Energy of Your Home, 177
Saint Thérèse of Lisieux, 2-4, 205-8
Salus, 190
Sanders, Barry, 147-48
Sarasvati, 37-39
Sekmet, 41, 196-97
Selene, 84-86
self-esteem, 99-102
Semans, Anne, 129
Serenity Prayer, 219
serpent, 190-91
Seth, 81-82
Sexy Mamas: Keeping Your Sex Life Alive While Raising Kids, 129
Shakti, 176
Shepard, Paul, 147-48
Shintoism, 193-94
Shiva, 144
Siegel, Bernie S., 192
simplicity, 205-8
sincerity, 164-66
solace, 209-12
Sophia, 214

Spear, William, 177
Spider, 48-52
spirituality, 213-17
spontaneity, 103-5
Spring, 186
Steinem, Gloria, 102
The Story of a Soul, 205
storytelling, 26-27
Sunflower, 189
support, 167-70
Susano-Wo, 193
Swallow, 61
Swan, 61
symbolic messages, 31

T

Thalia, 87
Themis, 77-79
Theseus, 74-75
Three Graces, 87-90, 133
Tiger, 176-78
Timeless Healing: The Power of Biology and Belief, 192
tobacco, 149
Tortoise, 158-60
transformation, 106-9
Tree of Life, 200

Trivia, 113–16

Trois Frères, 40

Trojan War, 167

Tsukiyomi-no-Mikoto, 193

U

Ursa Major and Minor, 147

V

Van Gogh, Vincent, 86

Vesta, 13

Virgin Mary, 7–8, 139–42, 188, 215

vision, 218–21

visualization, 22–24

W

Warner, Marina, 92

Warrior Women, 101

weaving, 48–49

Wharton, Edith, 195

When Things Fall Apart: Heart Advice for Difficult Times, 212

White Painted Woman, 223

White Shell Woman, 223

Winks, Cathy, 129

Wolf, 124–27

womanhood, 222–25

Woman's Prayer to the Rising Sun for a Newborn Girl, 225

Women Who Run with the Wolves, 126

Woolf, Virginia, 72

Wren, 62

writing, 24–26

Y

Yggdrasill, 201

yin/yang, 152, 154

Z

Zephyr, 186

Zeus, 53, 66, 135–36, 153, 210

Zimmer, Heinrich, 62